Git G. Noam
Editor-in-Chief

NEW DIRECTIONS FOR YOUTH DEVELOPMENT

Theory
Practice
Research

spring | 2008

Community Organizing and Youth Advocacy

Sarah Deschenes
Milbrey McLaughlin
Anne Newman

issue
editors

JOSSEY-BASS™
An Imprint of
WILEY

COMMUNITY ORGANIZING AND YOUTH ADVOCACY
Sarah Deschenes, Milbrey McLaughlin, Anne Newman (eds.)
New Directions for Youth Development, No. 117, Spring 2008
Gil G. Noam, Editor-in-Chief

Microfilm copies of issues and articles are available in 16mm and 35mm, as well as microfiche in 105mm, through University Microfilms Inc., 300 North Zeeb Road, Ann Arbor, Michigan 48106-1346.

NEW DIRECTIONS FOR YOUTH DEVELOPMENT (ISSN 1533-8916, electronic ISSN 1537-5781) is part of The Jossey-Bass Psychology Series and is published quarterly by Wiley Subscription Services, Inc., A Wiley Company, at Jossey-Bass, 989 Market Street, San Francisco, California 94103-1741. POSTMASTER: Send address changes to New Directions for Youth Development, Jossey-Bass, 989 Market Street, San Francisco, California 94103-1741.

SUBSCRIPTIONS cost $85.00 for individuals and $209.00 for institutions, agencies, and libraries. Prices subject to change. Refer to the order form that appears at the back of most volumes of this journal.

EDITORIAL CORRESPONDENCE should be sent to the Editor-in-Chief, Dr. Gil G. Noam, McLean Hospital, 115 Mill Street, Belmont, MA 02478.

Cover photograph by Vasiliki Varvaki

www.josseybass.com

Contents

Issue Editors' Notes

THIS VOLUME OF *New Directions for Youth Development* represents
new thinking about the ways in which youth and parents are
engaged in local reform, particularly education reform. Opportunities for youth and parents to have their voices heard are growing, and community organizations are helping them do so.
Because of the organizing and advocacy taking place through
community organizations, groups traditionally outside the political system are having a more significant impact on what happens
for local youth.

The articles in this volume examine ways in which organizations
advocate for and with youth—through youth organizing, parent
organizing, more traditional youth advocacy, and funding support.
Youth advocacy can be defined as efforts that are taking place on
behalf of youth, whereas youth and parent organizing consists of
efforts to engage individuals in social change, develop leadership,
and tackle issues that participants themselves identify. Youth advocacy also tends to focus on outcomes, while youth and parent organizing typically give significant attention to the process of engaging
people in collective action.

Advocacy organizations and community organizers of different
stripes work in a variety of ways to improve conditions for youth
in urban areas: they lobby to change policy, connect diverse institutions to serve youth, and help youth become advocates for themselves. The article authors find a range of ways that organizations
challenge policymakers and other leaders in urban areas to create
better schools, get more resources for youth in city budgets, and
educate local officials about the needs of young people.

NEW DIRECTIONS FOR YOUTH DEVELOPMENT, NO. 117, SPRING 2008 © WILEY PERIODICALS, INC.
Published online in Wiley InterScience (www.interscience.wiley.com) • DOI: 10.1002/yd.242

Most of the article authors use case studies to examine the work of advocacy organizations. In this volume are case studies written by organizational leaders and by observers. Some contain a single case, and others compare organizations. We can learn the benefits, barriers, and complexities of advocacy and organizing work through these close examinations of organizations working for and with youth on policy change. With their diversity of efforts and locales, these cases also build a broader base of knowledge about advocacy and organizing.

All of the articles in this volume address organizing and advocacy on a local level—the level at which policies and the needs of youth and families meet. As we describe in the first article, there is a local advantage to the work that community-based organizations do for and with youth. These organizations know about the needs and resources in their communities and can craft specific proposals to address them, forge strong local partnerships and coalitions around issues, and negotiate the particular mix of contexts in each setting.

The second and third articles take up local youth organizing for education reform and efforts to help youth become agents for change in their own school contexts. Mark R. Warren, Meredith Mira, and Thomas Nikundiwe provide an analysis of the recent rise in local youth organizing focused on school issues. Using case studies of two organizations, one working in Baltimore and one in Boston, they find a trajectory in the concerns of youth organizing groups from community issues to school reform. Seema Shah and Kavitha Mediratta also examine the impact of youth organizing on education reform efforts, focusing on the relationship between youth organizers and local educators and how issues of race and class are part of this work. They find three key strategies youth use to get their message heard and gain support from educators and school systems and suggest implications for reform efforts and educators.

NTanya Lee, the executive director of Coleman Advocates for Children and Youth in San Francisco, describes some significant changes in strategy that the organization has made over the past thirty years. This advocacy organization has recently begun to shift its structure and strategies toward a bottom-up community organizing model and is considering ways in which it can be more accountable to the communities of color it represents.

Michael P. Evans and Dennis Shirley in the fifth article and Ron Snyder in the sixth examine parent organizing for school reform in Boston and Oakland, respectively. Evans and Shirley examine parent participation in organizing, both traditional understandings and the developments they have studied in the Jamaica Plain Parent Organizing Project. They are interested in the moral imperative parents see in their organizing work, pushing for change for the whole community in addition to change for their own children, and how organizations might support this type of collective civic engagement. Snyder details the experience of Oakland Community Organizations (OCO) in bringing small schools to Oakland in response to community members' concerns about overcrowding and unsafe school conditions. He discusses OCO's organizing model, its partnerships, work inside and outside the system, and the role of the faith community.

Finally, Sylvia M. Yee describes the entrance of one San Francisco foundation, the Evelyn and Walter Haas, Jr. Fund, into the world of youth organizing: what it took to make that shift and how the foundation has understood the relationships between youth development and youth organizing. Yee also provides a guide for how other foundations can support youth advocacy and organizing.

Many of the article authors reflect on the larger impact of organizing on the participants, in addition to the concrete changes that have taken place. They note a shift from a self-interest frame to a larger understanding of the importance of civic engagement in communities (Warren, Mira, and Nikundiwe; Snyder; and Evans and Shirley). There is a ripple effect in these local youth and parent organizing efforts; not only do policies and contexts change, but groups and communities themselves begin to change too.

Although youth are still not central players in most of the policy decisions that affect their lives, the articles in this volume suggest that significant progress is being made to give youth and parents the tools and opportunities to improve schools and other institutions in their lives. And their organizing is having tangible results in many urban areas.

Sarah Deschenes
Milbrey McLaughlin
Anne Newman
Editors

SARAH DESCHENES *is a consultant who has been conducting research on education policy, community development, and out-of-school time for over a decade. She was also a postdoctoral fellow at the John W. Gardner Center for Youth and Their Communities at Stanford University.*

MILBREY MCLAUGHLIN *is the David Jacks Professor of Education and Public Policy at Stanford University, the founding director of the John W. Gardner Center for Youth and Their Communities, and the codirector of the Center for Research on the Context of Teaching.*

ANNE NEWMAN *is an assistant professor of education at Washington University in St. Louis, where her work focuses on educational philosophy and policy.*

Executive Summary

Chapter One: Organizations advocating for youth: The local advantage

Sarah Deschenes, Milbrey McLaughlin, Anne Newman

Youth occupy a unique place in our democratic society. They must primarily rely on others to speak on their behalf as decisions are made about the allocation of resources within and across various youth-serving institutions. Advocacy organizations comprise crucial representational assets for all youth, but America's poorest children and youth especially need an effective voice to speak for and about them. Yet advocates for youth in urban areas face tough challenges since urban voters typically have few positive connections to youth. This article draws on three years of research focused on three organizations in the San Francisco Bay Area that have successfully advocated for better policies for youth. The authors explore the strategies that these organizations have employed to overcome the challenges they face, with particular attention to the advantages that follow from advocating at the local rather than at the state or federal level.

NEW DIRECTIONS FOR YOUTH DEVELOPMENT, NO. 117, SPRING 2008 © WILEY PERIODICALS, INC.
Published online in Wiley InterScience (www.interscience.wiley.com) • DOI: 10.1002/yd.243

Chapter Two: Youth organizing: From youth development to school reform

Mark R. Warren, Meredith Mira, Thomas Nikundiwe

Over the past twenty years, youth organizing has grown across the country. Through organizing, young people identify issues of concern and mobilize their peers to build action campaigns to achieve their objectives. Youth organizing has been appreciated for its contributions to youth and community development. The authors use two case studies to trace the more recent emergence of youth organizing as an important force for school reform. The Boston-based Hyde Square Task Force began with a focus on afterschool programming, but its youth leaders now organize to get Boston Public Schools to adopt a curriculum addressing sexual harassment. Meanwhile, the Baltimore Algebra Project began as a peer-to-peer tutoring program but now also organizes to demand greater funding for Baltimore schools. These cases illustrate a broader phenomenon where students reverse the deficit paradigm by acting out of their own self-interest to become agents of institutional change.

Chapter Three: Negotiating reform: Young people's leadership in the educational arena

Seema Shah, Kavitha Mediratta

Youth organizing within the institutional context of community-based organizations has grown exponentially. Drawing on interviews with more than eighty organizers, youth, and educators, this article examines young people's experiences as they organize to expand educational opportunities for themselves and their peers in urban school districts. The authors explore educator responses to youth organizing and analyze how race- and class-based assumptions about youth leadership, as well as differing cultural norms between schools and youth organizing groups, pose challenges for young people fighting for education reform. The authors describe three strategies youth organizing groups use to address these challenges: intensive leadership development, targeted relationship building with district administrators, and alliance building. Implications for both educators and youth organizing groups are discussed.

Chapter Four: Thirty years of advocacy in San Francisco: Lessons learned and the next generation of leadership

NTanya Lee

Professional advocacy organizations are often challenged by the question of their authentic community representation and their ability to balance short-term pragmatism with strategic plans for long-term, systemic change. Coleman Advocates, one of the nation's most effective child advocacy organizations, has taken up this challenge under the leadership of a next-generation leader of color who followed a dynamic director of the baby boom generation. In this piece, Coleman's thirty years of social change strategies are analyzed from the perspective of this new executive director, who has facilitated the latest organizational shift that deepens its commitment to building bottom-up grassroots leadership and community power while keeping the best of the professional, staff-led advocacy model. Issues of race, accountability, power, and movement building are addressed through the lens of one organization's evolution, with the goal of building a long-term movement that will achieve racial and economic equity for all children and families.

Chapter Five: The development of collective moral leadership among parents through education organizing

Michael P. Evans, Dennis Shirley

It is often assumed that parent participation in schools is primarily based on self-interest and that this is a frequent source of contention between parents and teachers. This article examines the

NEW DIRECTIONS FOR YOUTH DEVELOPMENT • DOI: 10.1002/yd

experiences of members of the Jamaica Plain Parent Organizing Project (JP-POP), a community-based organization in Boston, and reveals that some parents have learned to act beyond their individual self-interest and to organize on behalf of the entire community as a result of their participation. The authors present qualitative data from interviews with JP-POP members to ascertain the motivations behind their initial decisions to become involved in education, the benefits they derive from their participation, and the gradual evolution of narrow definitions of self-interest to more communal understandings. Finally, they draw out implications for the potential capacity enhancement of community-based organizations in education at both the institutional and district levels.

Chapter Six: Faith-based organizing for youth: One organization's district campaign for small schools policy

Ron Snyder

Oakland Community Organizations (OCO) has worked for over ten years to improve educational opportunities in low-income neighborhoods in Oakland, California. The work of thousands of parent, teacher, youth, and community leaders has resulted in the formation of nearly fifty new small schools and more than ten charters, creating settings for individualized learning environments and the opportunity for quality choices for many of Oakland's low-income families. In this article, OCO's executive director, Ron Snyder, outlines a four-phase organizing process undertaken by OCO, based on a set of organizing principles that have sustained community-led education reform despite constant changes in the political and school district environment: the centrality of love (self-interest) as a motivator for advocacy; the importance of quality research and powerful ideas (vision) as alternatives to the status quo; application of a model that creates a common structure, language, and experience to sustain leaders; the need for institutional and network power to apply leverage; the flexibility to seize opportunity when the window is open; and faithfulness to the object of our love: our children.

Chapter Seven: Developing the field of youth organizing and advocacy: What foundations can do

Sylvia M. Yee

For more than a decade, the Evelyn and Walter Haas, Jr. Fund has seeded many San Francisco Bay Area youth organizing and advocacy programs. Now that the field is maturing, argues the fund's vice president of programs, foundations have a critical programmatic and capacity-building role to play. The author offers analysis and strategies for integrating youth development grant making across foundation interest areas. The programs described illustrate the diversity of youth organizing and advocacy programs that could be supported by funders, whether or not any particular philanthropic institution has a grant-making focus on youth development or youth organizing. The article ends with an in-depth portrait of the self-reported needs of youth organizing and advocacy programs and concrete strategies for foundations seeking to more effectively enable youth organizing and advocacy to play an important role in bringing about a more vibrant, diverse, and effective democratic culture.

Organizations advocating for and with urban youth negotiate many institutional settings to improve policies that shape youth's lives. This article considers three such organizations and the barriers and opportunities in their local environments.

1

Organizations advocating for youth: The local advantage

Sarah Deschenes, Milbrey McLaughlin, Anne Newman

HISTORY TEACHES THAT without effective political activism dedicated to their interests, poor and marginalized children are likely to lose in the competition for public resources. Youth growing up in the nation's urban centers face special challenges in making their voices heard and needs understood. For example, the increasing distance between the inner cities, where many of America's neediest youth grow up, and suburban communities, where the lion's share of political and financial resources sits, segregate urban youth and their parents.

Urban demographics also forecast political isolation. In the nation's urban centers, only around 15 percent of adult residents have children in the public school system, and so the voting population has scant direct investment in education and youth services.

This chapter draws on research carried out by the authors in collaboration with W. Richard Scott and Kathryn Hopkins and presented in the forthcoming book *Between Movement and Establishment: Organizations Advocating for Youth.*

NEW DIRECTIONS FOR YOUTH DEVELOPMENT, NO. 117, SPRING 2008 © WILEY PERIODICALS, INC.
Published online in Wiley InterScience (www.interscience.wiley.com) • DOI: 10.1002/yd.244

The interests of urban youth must compete for attention on a civic agenda with issues more compelling to voters—municipal transportation and public safety, for example. And urban voters typically have few positive connections to youth. Many encounter urban youth only on the evening news in stories of gang violence, school failures, teen pregnancy, or various forms of civic disrespect. The policy contexts surrounding youth thus range from benign acceptance, to indifference, to antagonism. Consequently urban youth, especially impoverished youth, are often politically marginalized and of little account in city halls when priorities are set.

Organizations advocating for and with urban youth have an uphill battle to fight. They confront barriers rooted in established ideas, society's institutions, and existing privilege. Given that most urban voters do not have children who rely on public resources, advocates working in these settings often find it difficult to arouse passion and mobilize action around youth. Ideas about urban youth—who they are, what they need, and who should provide it—play in the background of public and private deliberations about youth policies. Citizens, politicians, community leaders, and others have mental models of what youth-focused institutions such as schools and the role of government should be. These value-based, contextual, and institutional issues present youth advocates tough challenges, since in urban areas, neither the direct self-interest of powerful organizational players nor warrant for public investments consistent with a youth development perspective is particularly obvious or especially compelling.

Yet even in the face of this difficult reality, organizations advocating for youth negotiate this array of institutional constraints in their local community settings, using their knowledge of local players, crafting specific proposals around local issues, and developing relationships across sectors to change policy. We draw on three years of research in the San Francisco Bay Area to show that organizations advocating for youth can play a strategic role in advancing policies and relationships that provide positive supports and opportunities for urban youth. We describe the advantage of organizations that advocate for and with youth and their families at the local rather than at the state or national level.

NEW DIRECTIONS FOR YOUTH DEVELOPMENT • DOI: 10.1002/yd

Diverse ways of making a difference

Coleman Advocates for Children and Youth in San Francisco, the San Francisco Organizing Project (SFOP), and Oakland Community Organizations (OCO) are three local organizations that have successfully managed the extraordinarily difficult task of mobilizing support across fractured, segmented interests to bring about new and different resources for youth in their communities.[1] The strategies provide information about current problems, engender support around common values and normative agendas, and invent novel ways to attack issues.

Oakland Community Organizations and SFOP are community organizing groups that see their primary goal as leadership development, enabling those affected by policies to play a more active role in shaping them. These members of the PICO National Network, a network of community-building organizations, view their broader mission as working to revive participatory democracy by encouraging individual involvement within neighborhoods. These organizations are as concerned with altering how policies are determined—with process—as with what policy decisions are made—policy outcomes. Their commitment to leadership development, largely in the form of parent organizing, puts residents in charge of executing campaigns. Although the policy solutions that members propose are often not what an expert might advise, as SFOP's director suggests, they reflect both the interests and actions of those most affected by the outcomes.

Coleman Advocates also seeks to train youth and parents to define and pursue issues of interest to them through its empowerment groups, Youth Making a Change (YMAC), and parent groups that focus on housing and education reform. Although these empowerment groups have been an important part of Coleman's structure since the mid-1990s, Coleman has traditionally focused more on policy change than on leadership development. Its structure has historically placed primary responsibility for the design and execution of advocacy efforts on its professional staff. This greater reliance on professional staff to select and pursue campaign issues has enabled Coleman to employ politically effective strategies and seize opportunities for reform. Under its current leadership, however, Coleman is moving toward a more empowerment-focused model that is closer to the structure of OCO and SFOP.

These three organizations seek to improve the opportunities afforded the youth of their communities and influence public policy directly. For example, OCO's work to promote small schools in Oakland changed the education policy landscape in that city; the passage of the New Small Autonomous Schools Policy prompted the creation of fifteen new small schools in Oakland and restructured two existing high schools.[2] Similarly, Coleman directly influenced public policy in San Francisco by drafting and promoting the Children's Amendment, which has dedicated a portion of the city's tax revenue to children and youth programs since its passage in 1991 and reauthorization in 2000. And although SFOP's small schools campaign in San Francisco initially had a rocky time engaging the school district, its efforts resulted in the opening of a new school, focused community attention on small schools as a way to improve public education, and eventually led to the passage of a school board resolution to develop a small schools policy. All of these represent successful efforts by three organizations to improve the lives of thousands of youth in their communities through public policy reform.

We next turn to how these organizations achieved these policy triumphs, with particular attention to the environments and opportunities at the local level that contributed to their success.

The local advantage

Organizations advocating for and with youth at any level of government almost always assume a challenger's stance, pushing for change in existing policies, practices, and institutional arrangements. Engaging these challenges on behalf of youth necessarily embroils advocacy organizations in the age-old dialectic between advocates for change and supporters of the status quo. Political actors, be they stand-patters or challengers, try to manage the discourse around a policy issue by means of rhetoric, symbols, and analysis.[3] Much of advocates' work involves the same.

Rhetorical opposition

In order for organizations to be successful in these campaigns, they must assuage worries that soft approaches to troubled teens will promote more crime and violence (perverse outcomes arguments), respond to conserving positions that view expanded investments in youth as futile since the problems of urban youth are intractable (futility arguments), and effectively counter claims that new resources and opportunities for marginalized youth will jeopardize the elite's privilege or resources available to adults (jeopardy arguments).[4]

Our focal organizations generally prevailed in managing the rhetoric surrounding youth issues in their communities, largely because they did so in language and terms meaningful to local politicians, voters, and officials. Negative outcomes, our focal advocacy organizations argued, would follow not from the youth development stance they advanced but instead from existing get-tough policies that pushed youth out of school, onto the streets, and into the juvenile justice system. Advocates presented data to show that once youth are in "the system," few reconnect with positive pathways; instead they return to crime and, eventually, adult prison. Advocates argued that the most promising strategies for connecting troubled urban youth to positive futures lie in approaches that highlight positive youth development and focus on ways youth can stay connected to schools, families, and the workforce. In a setting where bigger prison facilities and stricter antigang policies were being pushed by a powerful segment of the Oakland community and Alameda County, OCO countered these sentiments with facts. To advance their small schools agenda, for example, OCO used research documenting the successful youth outcomes associated with the small schools model it was promoting in Oakland.

Advocates countered futility arguments by highlighting counterexamples. OCO drew on student experiences in their successful small schools to feature instances where reformed school environments enabled at-risk youth to reimagine their futures and begin to succeed in school. Oakland Community Organizations also addressed futility concerns with data. In Oakland, school officials risked additional public embarrassment if they ignored the stark evidence of the educational inequalities OCO presented in public forums by showing the differences between better-resourced hilltop and more impoverished flatland schools in the city. Oakland Community Organizations turned threat into opportunity by providing a clear, well-thought-out course of action grounded in research.

Youth advocates upended the jeopardy argument, turning politicians' concerns about political peril from "damned if you do" to "damned if you don't." The political pressure they brought to bear constituted clear risks to city hall and elected officials should they neglect or obstruct advocacy organizations' youth agenda. Coleman used politicians' public statements of commitment to youth—delivered while campaigning—to hold them accountable. What politician wants to be portrayed as breaking promises to the city's children and youth? In this way, Coleman recast the inherent political liability of urban youth (they and their parents do not vote) into a political asset (the community has a moral obligation to its most vulnerable citizens).

These examples of advocates' responses to rhetorical opposition underscore the ways in which advocacy at the local level—the rhetoric, symbols, and actions employed—differs from that operating at other levels of the policy system. To be sure, local contexts are vulnerable to policies originating at state and national levels. The high-stakes accountability measures contained in the current federal education act, No Child Left Behind, for instance, has led to a laser-like focus on student achievement that crowds out significant attention to youth development outcomes more broadly conceived. Nonetheless, local organizations operate in an environment distinctly different from the settings that advocates face at state and national levels. At the national level, politics are deeply partisan, and ideas often serve as "weapons of mass persuasion."[5] For example, the prominent 1983 report on American education, *A Nation at Risk*, famously mobilized Congress and state policymakers to increase education spending under the threat that a "rising tide of mediocrity" would cost the United States dearly in the global economic race.[6] By contrast, mobilizing support at the local level relies less on ideological, partisan persuasion and more on specific appeals to concrete action. What should the community do for its youth? What can the community do for its youth? What do youth need? In several ways, then, local advocates' rhetoric and action differ from those found at higher levels of government. Here we explore some of these differences and the advantages that follow from them.

Specific proposals and concrete actions

Local advocates are advantaged by deep social and political knowledge of their context. This asset enables them to build cases especially persuasive in their setting by virtue of situated evidence and arguments. Advocates articulated a "logic of appropriateness," or what individuals consider appropriate in a particular social, political, and institutional context.[7]

Advocates at the local level can reference details of past bargains, specific contexts, and consequences to marshal support for their cause. "Institutional memory of how to effectively move the system," said Coleman's former executive director, "is what has helped sustain [Coleman's] effectiveness." Known personalities, familiar positions, and concrete tasks shape the discourse and argumentation of local advocacy organizations. And local youth have names, faces, and connections to community institutions; they are not hypothetical "American youth" failing to "meet standards." Coleman, OCO, and SFOP successfully assembled scores of youth to march in front of city hall, attend school board meetings, and meet with the media. These youth were undeniably of the community.

Our cases also show how local reformers can mobilize support when they are able to point to specific action and local consequences. In so doing, local advocates offset what Hojnacki and colleagues call the "uncertainty advantage" that status quo defenders use to erode support for change.[8] What would it look like? What would it cost? Who would benefit? Best to stick to the known, argue the defenders. Each focal organization constructed compelling arguments designed to change public ideas about youth and community responsibilities for them. All compiled data that detailed youth's needs and the inadequate resources currently available, and crafted well-supported proposals for change in clear, evidence-based terms.

Advocates are aware of their local advantage. As Coleman's former executive director put it, "The localness of it is one of the things that has kept us innovative and me interested all of these years. . . . It is very easy to translate [goals into action], to have both contact with the people that you're trying to see things changed for as well as the systems you're trying to change." In this way, localness can shift rhetoric from the ideologically based contentions heard at state and national levels to alternative proposals for immediate action, pictured and pitched in local terms.

Relationships and coalitions

Local organizations' dexterity and political power draw heavily on the coalitions they can assemble, often on short notice, to lobby for an issue. Coleman's policy triumphs are often rooted in its long-standing relationships with city officials and agencies—relationships it persistently cultivates and then draws on to achieve its reform goals by calling on its "kid-friendly" allies and challenging its detractors. Coleman acted as a broker and convener, creating new coalitions and relationships to press for a youth agenda and policy change. "It is about grooming and building coalitions," said the former executive director. Coleman exploited relational mechanisms to bring pressure on policymakers and elected officials, which created an effective voice for change and action. These relationships changed depending on specific issues and key people; the organization's powerful connections enabled bricolage and flexible assembly of politically consequential supporters. These relationships built on the organization's broad acceptance and credibility in the community. Coleman's strong social capital made the organization both a threat and a positive collaborator in the youth policy arena.

SFOP and OCO, in their roles as community organizers, enlisted and enabled member congregations to speak to power through their political presence. They built local grassroots capacity for political change and alternative mechanisms for political expression by assembling constituents through relationships of trust. By empowering citizens, SFOP and OCO opened up the policymaking process to otherwise marginalized voices and worked to make public officials accountable to all of their constituents. SFOP's executive director put her organization's mission this way: "It's about reclaiming and revitalizing democracy. . . . building a strong democracy . . . where ordinary people are really engaged in running the country." SFOP and OCO's capacity to quickly mobilize and register voters through their member churches confronted elected officials and community elites with the collective voice of citizens.

These effective relationships are local relationships, ties that feature multiple connections and interlocking loyalties. This kind of social and political capital supporting youth advocacy and organizing efforts has a distinctly local character and roots. According to Coleman's former director, "You can only do it at the local level. . . . You just have the proximity of people . . . when you're shut out of the mayor's office or someplace, you make connections with someone who isn't shut out. It's all about being good politicians." SFOP and OCO, operating according to PICO's organizing principle of "no permanent enemies, no permanent allies," have been able to mobilize coalitions around support for specific issues rather than ideological affiliation or former position. SFOP's director says, "We have that niche and that credibility of representing a very wide base and being nonpartisan, being a more moderate voice. I think one of our greatest strengths is that we really are not seen as one side or the other."

Range of action

Advocates for youth at state and national levels typically specialize in a particular policy area or institution: health, juvenile justice, special education, or school finance, for example. Rarely do these advocates venture outside their domain of expertise to consider youth issues more broadly. For individuals engaged in youth advocacy and organizing at the local level, opportunities exist to work across youth-serving sectors to address youth needs comprehensively. The Department of Children, Youth and Their Families in San Francisco, for instance, is a product of Coleman's efforts to integrate and coordinate the city's health and human services for youth. This wide range possible at the local level is what kept policy entrepreneurs like Coleman's former executive director energized and focused on the broader picture for youth. In the course of a week when she led Coleman Advocates, for example, she met with an array of individuals affecting youth policies: pediatricians, school officials, neighborhood parent groups, the local media, foundation program officers, and the heads of various city departments. And if one agency or official is not receptive, local advocates can approach another for support. The narrower scope of advocacy work in Sacramento or Washington, D.C., she says, "isn't anywhere near as interesting" as what she could tackle and potentially accomplish for youth in San Francisco.

Local advocates are also able to adjust the scope of action to suit the local comfort zone and build support for their cause one step at a time. And because it is more confined than state or national policy settings, the local context also allows an incremental approach to change and permits advocates to address their goals through successive approximation rather than major legislation or policy change. SFOP deliberately pursued this strategy with its small schools campaign by starting with one school and educating district officials along the way—activities that finally resulted in passage of a school board resolution supporting small schools. Small wins can add up to significant change in policy and practice at the local level because they can demonstrate to naysayers that the proposed change did not result in the anticipated negative consequences and because proximity to practice permits midcourse corrections and adaptations.

Advocates as educators

Local advocates and organizers also can be educators in ways difficult to accomplish at national and state levels by teaching local leaders and politicians about the needs of youth and promising practices through direct experience and contacts. Leaders of our case organizations see coalition building as a fundamental educational task, teaching community members and others about the nature of an issue and possible responses. And that education can be hands-on, locally meaningful in both process and consequence. Oakland Community Organizations' director and others in the organization spent countless hours briefing school board members and other public officials about their plans, in the process getting them on board before crucial votes were taken on the small schools project. Staff at SFOP had numerous meetings with the superintendent of schools, the mayor, school board members, county supervisors, and others, and they show up regularly at gatherings where issues of interest are discussed. Coleman met with San Francisco mayor Gavin Newsom just as he was coming into office, drove him around the city to see the conditions of local parks, and provided him a thorough education on youth issues.

Coleman also sees its educator role in terms of informing politicians headed for the state level about youth issues and policy opportunities. For example, Coleman worked closely with California assemblyman Mark Leno when he was a member of the San Francisco County Board of Supervisors, encouraging him to support youth-friendly measures in areas such as universal health care for children and attention to childhood obesity. Leno took those interests with him when he went to Sacramento in 2002 and provides effective backing for policies benefiting youth.

Local context matters: Precipitating events and enabling factors

Coleman, SFOP, and OCO are not unique in adopting roles as urban educators, brokers, or organizers to advance a youth agenda and neutralize rhetoric harmful to their cause. Nor are they unique in crafting specific proposals keyed to local contexts. But they have been arguably more successful than many similar organizations working for youth in urban settings. Factors operating in their larger political context influenced their ability to succeed where advocates using similar tactics in other environments have come up short. Mechanisms operating in their immediate environment shaped both the opportunities for and the contributions of our focal organizations.

Ideas and concrete plans of action matter most in conditions of crisis and upheaval. Oakland schools were in crisis and heading for state takeover as OCO was mounting its campaign for small, autonomous schools. Oakland Community Organizations proposed a clear, well-substantiated alternative in the context of state pressure for the district to turn around its failing schools. Its campaign had a major impact in Oakland and earned the organization a national reputation for spearheading one of the few community-based school reform initiatives to take hold in a large urban area.

No such precipitating event animated change in education policies in San Francisco, and as a consequence, in part, SFOP has not been equally successful with its similar small schools campaign. Its small schools campaign in San Francisco has just begun to make progress after more than five years. The campaign resulted in the opening of one new small school, and the city adopted a small schools policy in February 2007. The Oakland context of school crisis enabled OCO's pursuit of equity to override the district's commitment to professional authority and bureaucratic efficiencies much more quickly. SFOP faced a more stable and entrenched school bureaucracy in San Francisco, which made its reform goals harder to pursue.

A more broad-based environmental factor facilitated Coleman's work: concern over the flight of families from San Francisco. Coleman's slogan, "San Francisco is better with children," struck a chord with the electorate and received public endorsement from Mayor Newsom and others with local influence. Youth-focused policies aimed at better health care, recreation, and other social supports garnered voter support not only because of Coleman's moral message about social obligation but also because of the alarming decline of the number of youth in the city. Not just white, advantaged families are leaving San Francisco; the city has experienced the steepest drop in its black population of any other major American city.[9] Coleman leveraged this community decline into an issue requiring attention and promotes proposals to make the city a viable place for families.

NEW DIRECTIONS FOR YOUTH DEVELOPMENT • DOI: 10.1002/yd

Both SFOP and Coleman used another particular San Francisco feature to their advantage: the extraordinary number of commissions in San Francisco and the transparency required by the city's especially strict Sunshine Ordinance.[10] In one sense, this feature of local politics makes change slow. According to one observer and SFOP adviser, these factors are "effective largely in stopping things. . . . It tends to be easier to advocate to stop something than to get something going because then you get the next group who is saying, no, no, no!" But the upside of having many commissions is that organizations have more opportunities to voice their concerns in official public forums. SFOP has used this feature to achieve its goals because it "can get the troops out . . . to show up at 6 o'clock next Tuesday at the health commission to protest."

Precipitating events and enabling factors in both communities provide explanation for the outcomes achieved by our focal advocacy organizations. Ideas take hold close to the ground, and local advocates can keep a weather eye out for shifts in the institutional or political context and for new actors sympathetic to their message. As SFOP's director told us, "We as organizers are always looking for what are the political windows of opportunity and that's in part why we are doing some of our own reconnaissance and meeting with people, and reading and trying to figure out what those might be."

These environmental factors underscore the influence of the local political context as yet another source of complexity in understanding these organizations' work. The significance of local context is also a barrier to generalizing across settings about the implications of organizations' design and strategies. But the significance of these elements also points out ways in which the local context can present the most significant opportunities for organizations advocating for youth. Local politics, institutions, and relationships afford youth advocates and organizers opportunities for actions that differ from those at other levels in terms of their immediacy and concreteness. They also call for rhetoric and symbols directly meaningful in their local context. Conceptions and expressions of effective advocacy, then, vary not only across local settings but also across levels of government.

Conclusion

Young people grow up in communities, not in programs or categorical initiatives, and local decisions about the resources associated with youth-focused policies and programs, be they national, state, or local in origin, ultimately matter the most. Communities are the settings in which the situated and specific needs of youth can be understood and addressed; they are the places where professionals, politicians, and civic leaders can establish priorities for investments in their young people, define locally meaningful indicators of positive outcomes, and integrate resources across sectors, agencies, and age groups. Moreover, decades of implementation research demonstrate that despite the regulatory structures, mandates, and other trappings that accompany categorical state and federal policies, the policy that ultimately matters most is the one made by local interpretation and response.[11]

For all of these reasons, although state and national advocacy groups can prod lawmakers to pass legislation favoring youth, local advocacy organizations and community organizers can make the most difference in how resources are provided to youth, the coherence of and support for a local youth agenda, and decision makers' responsiveness to local needs. Local organizations can keep local leadership who are focused on youth aware of pressing concerns and shortfalls and accountable to promises made.

Notes

1. San Francisco Organizing Project and OCO are not advocacy organizations in the sense that Coleman Advocates is; they are community organizing groups that focus on diverse issues, including youth. We include them here as advocacy organizations because their organizing activities comprise advocacy for young people in their communities.

2. As of October 6, 2006; see http://www.oaklandcommunity.org/issues.html.

3. See Baumgartner, F. R., & Jones, B. D. (1991). Agenda dynamics and policy subsystems. *Journal of Politics, 53*(4), 1044–1074.

4. See Hirschman, A. O. (1991). *The rhetoric of reaction.* Cambridge, MA: Harvard University Press.

5. Beland, D. (2005). *Social security: History and politics from the New Deal to the privatization debate.* Lawrence: University Press of Kansas. P. 28.

6. National Commission for Excellence in Education. (1983). *A nation at risk: The imperatives for educational reform.* Washington, DC: Author.
7. March, J. G., & Olsen, J. P. (1989). *Rediscovering institutions.* New York: Free Press.
8. Hojnacki, M., Baumgartner, F. R., Berry, J. M., Kimball, D. C., & Leech, B. L. (2006, August–September). *Goals, salience, and the nature of advocacy.* Paper presented at the annual meeting of the American Political Science Association, Philadelphia.
9. Yogis, J. (2006, September). What happened to blacks in San Francisco? *San Francisco.* Retrieved from http://www.sanfranciscomagazine.com/archives/view_story/1394/.
10. "The Sunshine Ordinance is an ordinance to insure easier access to public records and to strengthen the open meeting laws. The Sunshine Ordinance also outlines a procedure for citizens to follow if they do not receive public records they have requested." http://www.ci.sf.ca.us/site/bdsupvrs_index.asp?id=22269.
11. Pressman, J., & Wildavsky, A. (1973). *Implementation: How great expectations in Washington are dashed in Oakland, or, why it's amazing that federal programs work at all.* Berkeley: University of California Press; McLaughlin, M. W. (2006). Implementation research in education: Lessons learned, lingering questions and new opportunities. In M. I. Honig (Ed.), *New directions in education policy implementation: Confronting complexity.* Albany: State University of New York Press.

SARAH DESCHENES *is a consultant who has been conducting research on education policy, community development, and out-of-school time for over a decade. She was also a postdoctoral fellow at the John W. Gardner Center for Youth and Their Communities at Stanford University.*

MILBREY MCLAUGHLIN *is the David Jacks Professor of Education and Public Policy at Stanford University, the founding director of the John W. Gardner Center for Youth and Their Communities, and the codirector of the Center for Research on the Context of Teaching.*

ANNE NEWMAN *is an assistant professor of education at Washington University in St. Louis, where her work focuses on educational philosophy and policy.*

Case studies in Boston and Baltimore provide two examples of the emergence of youth organizing as a force for school reform, in addition to its better-known role as a contributor to positive developmental outcomes for young people.

2

Youth organizing: From youth development to school reform

Mark R. Warren, Meredith Mira, Thomas Nikundiwe

OVER THE PAST TWENTY YEARS, a new movement of young people has begun to grow across the country. In these efforts of youth organizing, young people work collectively to identify issues of concern and mobilize their peers to build action campaigns for achieving their objectives. Working with adult mentors, they learn about processes of social change and build power to create positive change in their lives. Scholars and practitioners have shown interest in youth organizing for its positive effects on youth and community development.[1] But few people have noticed a more recent trend in youth organizing: youth taking action for school reform.[2] From this point of view, youth organizing is important not just for its developmental outcomes for the young people themselves. It is emerging as a powerful force for improving schools in many inner-city communities.

Until recently, most youth organizing efforts took place mainly around issues young people faced in the communities in which they lived.[3] More recently, many youth organizing groups have focused their attention on the state of the education they are receiving, particularly in high schools. One study showed that by the early 2000s, there were literally hundreds of youth organizing efforts across the country, and 75 percent of them addressed education reform in some way.[4] Moreover, many of these efforts had expanded to district-level significance. In Los Angeles, South Central Youth Empowered thru Action allied with InnerCity Struggle and other groups to spearhead a campaign for providing college preparatory courses at all district high schools.[5] Meanwhile, Californians for Justice, a statewide alliance of youth organizations, organized to win a two-year delay in the implementation of the state's mandatory high school exit exams.[6]

What is youth organizing?

By "youth organizing," we mean an approach that "trains young people in community organizing and advocacy and helps them use these skills to alter power relations and create meaningful institutional change in their communities."[7] We can distinguish youth organizing from two better-known types of youth work: youth services and youth advocacy. In the typical approach of youth programming, services are provided for young people; youth are clients. In organizing, youth are seen as agents of change. Organizing efforts assist youth to come together collectively, decide which issues they will pursue, and build the power necessary to achieve their aims. Advocacy groups tend to be adult-dominated organizations that advocate for young people, such as the Children's Defense Fund. Youth organizing groups, by contrast, focus on the development of leadership among young people so that they can undertake direct action around issues and campaigns they themselves develop.

Youth organizing finds its origins in American traditions of community organizing. Although we can trace the roots of community organizing back to settlement house, populist, and other grassroots movements, the field began as a distinct approach through the work of Saul Alinsky in Chicago neighborhoods during the era of the Great Depression. Alinsky worked to organize working-class people to build power for themselves in their own neighborhoods.[8] Youth organizing efforts have centered among youth of color, who also draw from the traditions of youth participation in the civil rights movement and the Chicano movement, among others.[9] Civil rights leaders from the 1960s, like Ella Baker and Septima Clark, worked closely with local people to develop political consciousness and action from the ground up, tie local organizing efforts to the national movement, and mentor the young organizers conducting the early lunch counter sit-ins and later campaigns in the Student Nonviolent Coordinating Committee.[10]

Partly because of these influences, youth organizing typically features several distinguishing characteristics as compared to most adult community organizing. While Alinsky and his adult followers have been stubbornly pragmatic, youth organizers explicitly highlight the development of political consciousness among young people. Adult community organizing groups tend to avoid framing their work in racial terms, whereas youth organizing efforts often talk explicitly about their racial identity, and many see their work as addressing structural racism.

Much of the interest in youth organizing has focused on its impact on youth development. Youth organizing is seen as contributing to young people's interpersonal capacity, that is, their sense of belonging and self-worth.[11] It also influences civic participation. The focus on leadership development increases such civic skills as critical thinking, public speaking, planning, and group dynamics.[12] It also fosters the development of social and political consciousness, and it cultivates a sense of social responsibility and agency and a habit of participation that is likely to extend into adult life.[13]

Although observers have noted that youth organizing contributes to change in communities, few people have paid much attention to youth organizing as a force for school reform in low-income communities.[14] In part, this may be because youth organizing runs so counter to the dominant paradigm in the field of education. Young people are often portrayed as apathetic about their education, as students who must be motivated to learn. Worse, low-income students of color can be seen as incapable of learning at high levels or as disruptors who must be controlled.[15] Youth organizing provides a place for students to develop a counternarrative to failure, building their own sense of themselves as capable human beings.[16]

Over the past twenty years, adult-based community organizing groups have increasingly turned their attention to public education, typically focused at the elementary level.[17] Youth organizing has stepped into the secondary school vacuum. Young people acting to improve their high schools can be understood from the theoretical perspective of organizing, which has the notion of self-interest at its core.[18] Young people and their families represent the stakeholders with the strongest self-interest in receiving a high-quality education. In other words, by participating in organizing campaigns, youth act on their self-interest for the betterment of their own lives.

Self-interest should not be interpreted narrowly as selfishness or individualism. Organizers appreciate that young people's understandings of their self-interest can grow and develop through participation. As young people build relationships, talk with each other about their values and the issues they face, they build some shared understandings and a sense of common interests. Through educational programs and their own research, they learn about the social and political structures surrounding their communities so that they can set personal experience in relationship to institutional structures. Through working together on common projects, they strengthen their sense of collective identity and build power to achieve their shared agenda.

We now turn to two case studies of recent youth organizing efforts to address education reform. Two of the authors, Meredith Mira and Thomas Nikundiwe, conducted participant observation over a three-month period in the fall of 2006 with Boston's Hyde

Square Task Force, and one author, Thomas Nikundiwe, conducted participant observation at the Baltimore Algebra Project over a two-year period. We also conducted interviews with key participants at each organization and analyzed organizational documents. We combined and compared data from these sources in order to present an integrated analysis of each group.

Hyde Square Task Force: "Education and Community in Action"

The Hyde Square Task Force (HSTF), a youth organizing group located in the Boston neighborhood of Jamaica Plain, has served as a revitalizing force for the neighborhood since its inception in 1991. Its youth community organizers (YCOs) are teenagers who are actively involved in the decision-making processes that influence their lives. For most of the program's life, YCOs focused on community issues and claimed a number of significant accomplishments. More recently, the YCOs have turned their attention to Boston's school system.

Origins of the Hyde Square Task Force

The influx of immigrants and the building of public housing developments in the early twentieth century made the Hyde Square neighborhood of Boston a diverse urban community. However, by the early 1970s, the neighborhood had become better known for petty crimes, arson, stolen cars, and vandalism. In the 1980s, conditions became so bad that by the end of the decade, Boston police had dubbed Hyde Square the "cocaine capital of Boston." In response, a diverse group of neighbors organized to reclaim the streets of Hyde/Jackson Square. Activists recognized at that time that the only way to break the cycle of violence would be through sustained efforts to engage young people in the predominantly low-income Latino community. Throughout the 1990s, the HSTF worked to create a variety of afterschool programs to foster youth development.

Youth community organizers: From youth development to organizing

The HSTF moved toward organizing in 1999 when it established the YCO position as part of the Youth First in Jackson Square Initiative. Kmart had proposed building a big-box store on several acres of vacant land in the middle of the Jackson Square neighborhood. With the guidance of an adult organizer, Caprice Taylor Mendez, a group of fifteen teenagers at the HSTF met repeatedly to discuss the proposal and decided that the land could be better used as a youth and community center instead of a Kmart.

The group moved quickly to launch an organizing campaign for a community center. They joined forces with local merchants and affordable housing advocates who also objected to the Kmart development; together, they mobilized supporters, spoke at city hall public hearings, wrote letters to local newspapers, and hosted community forums. The YCOs held approximately fifty bilingual meetings with more than five hundred community residents. They organized a march and rally with over two hundred youth and adults on the vacant land where the Kmart was proposed. Finally, after several years of hard work and dedication to their cause, the youth won their campaign.

The current campaign: Sexual harassment in schools

Fresh from their victory, young people subsequently organized to change the voting age on the Jamaica Plain Neighborhood Council so that youth could serve on the body, and they also launched successful campaigns to improve parks and playgrounds in their neighborhood. This exclusive focus on community would begin to change, however, through the development of an ambitious sexual harassment campaign. In the summer of 2005, female YCOs decided that they were fed up with being sexually harassed as they walked from the Jackson Square subway station to the HSTF office on Centre Street.[19] To address the issue, the YCOs designed a bilingual sexual harassment card that they handed out to men on the street. The front of card read, "Stop Sexual Harassment . . . Please Treat Me with Respect . . . If It's Unwelcome, It's Sexual Harassment," and the back listed the offensive behaviors that qualify as harassment. After announcing the campaign at a well-attended press conference in August 2005, both male and female YCOs continued to create visibility around the issue with improvisational street theater. Their performances enabled the youth to explore their own issues around sexual harassment and educate their peers and the public on the subject. The young men were just as involved in the campaign efforts as were the women. Many of the men did not initially identify sexual harassment as a problem that they personally had experienced. However, through conversations with female YCOs, they came to see how sexual harassment influenced their own lives and the lives of their family members. As one former YCO noted, "From a male perspective, I am asking other men to stand up when others are being disrespectful. I want them to think about this—that woman that you are harassing and being disrespectful to could be your mother, sister, or cousin. Would you want that to happen to them?"[20]

As the YCOs learned more about sexual harassment, they realized that to address the issue fully, they had to move beyond their neighborhood-based campaign and tackle the issue within the Boston Public Schools (BPS). With the help of a doctoral student, the youth designed a survey that they distributed to five hundred students across ten high schools throughout Boston. The results showed that 80 percent of students in BPS, both male and female, had experienced some form of sexual harassment, defined by the YCOs as any unwanted touching, pinching, or grabbing by other students or teachers. The survey also showed that one in four students did not know how or to whom to report the incident.[21] After presenting these alarming statistics, the YCOs made three key demands. They wanted BPS to establish a new sexual harassment reporting system, adopt a new sex education curriculum that would include discussion of sexual harassment, and make the prevention of sexual harassment a priority for BPS.

The YCOs identified the deputy superintendent of teaching and learning, Chris Coxon, as their key target. Following a formal meeting with YCOs in July 2006, Coxon agreed to the three-part plan and committed to having three individuals from BPS work with the YCOs. The youth then held a six-hour weekend strategy session, where they developed their short- and long-term goals; identified the key players in the field, including their targets, allies, and opponents; and agreed on their overall strategy and associated tactics. To date, the YCOs continue to work with key members of BPS to ensure that they fulfill their demands.

Education organizing in the Boston context

Community organizations have found Boston a difficult place to do organizing around school issues because the district lacks neighborhood schools. Although 90 percent of YCOs go to school outside their neighborhood zones, the HSTF has been able to turn this situation to its advantage. Jesús Gerena, director of community development and organizing at the HSTF, stated, "The fact that we do have representation from so many schools around the city is a plus—it allows us to take on the system. And it's powerful for students because they get to go right to the top and deal with the decision makers." However, the YCOs have gained this access only because the HSTF had previously built a strong organizing base and experienced multiple wins at the neighborhood level, thereby gaining legitimacy among BPS officials. As one YCO said, "Before, they didn't care about young people; they thought that we were the cause of all of the problems. Now they're seeing that we have information that's useful for them." This type of youth involvement helps to create a counternarrative to the idea that youth are problems or risks; instead, they are beginning to be seen as agents who are creating positive education reforms.

Emboldened by their progress in their sexual harassment campaign, YCOs are now turning their attention to reforming the BPS civics curriculum. The HSTF's new focus on education reform has not meant that the group has abandoned its community-based work. The young people intend to continue such neighborhood campaigns as increasing the number of jobs for youth, decreasing violence, and increasing civic engagement. As one YCO aptly concluded, "We try to maintain a balance between our new efforts focusing on citywide schools and our neighborhood efforts. We have to have this neighborhood organizing as a basic part of our work. We're Jamaica Plain."

Baltimore Algebra Project: "Working the Demand Side of the Equation"

Civil rights leader Bob Moses[22] founded the Algebra Project in the 1980s as he came to think of math literacy as the key issue in the continuing struggle for citizenship and equality for people of color.[23] Inspired by Moses, Baltimore teacher Jay Gillen called ten Baltimore high school students to a meeting in his kitchen. In 2000, the group launched the Baltimore Algebra Project as a peer-to-peer math tutoring program, which came to serve four hundred students across the city. By 2003, the students had produced such an effective tutoring project that they successfully negotiated a sixty thousand dollar contract with the Baltimore City Public School System (BCPSS) to provide tutoring to middle school students.

Gillen always intended that students would take some kind of collective action as a group. He helped students develop the first two tiers of what Bob Moses calls a three-tier demand: demand on self, demand on others, and demand on society.[24] He told the students that once they made a demand on themselves, they could legitimately make a demand on their peers (the second tier) to join them in an effort to place a demand on the greater society. However, he never imagined an opportunity to organize would arrive so quickly.

When a budget crisis hit BCPSS in the 2003–2004 school year, BAP's tutoring program was one of the first to be cut. The students mobilized. While conducting research, students discovered a court case, *Bradford* v. *Maryland State Board of Education*, where Judge Joseph H. H. Kaplan had ordered the state of Maryland to provide Baltimore schools with an additional $200 million per year in funding.[25] But the state had effectively ignored the 2000 ruling and had not paid any of the money owed. Yet BAP students knew only too well how much the Baltimore school district needed these funds, as problems of perennial teacher shortages, outdated facilities, and insufficient instructional supplies plagued the system. Shocked by what they saw as the state's arrogant intransigence in the face of the need, the students turned their attention away from BCPSS and toward the state to demand compliance with the court's ruling.

From tutors to community leaders

The BAP students swung into action in the spring of 2004. They rallied over seven hundred students to protest the funding shortage in a series of walkouts and rallies in downtown Baltimore. They accomplished this mobilization by calling on their tutoring and personal networks, passing out thousands of fliers, and acquiring radio time to issue public calls for participation. In response, the judge asked two BAP students to participate in a special session with the case stakeholders. Later that summer, when the judge reopened hearings on the original 2000 ruling, he called BAP students as expert witnesses. The students submitted a petition with five hundred signatures demanding the judge hold the state in contempt of court.

Getting political

In October 2004, BAP students decided to target Nancy Grasmick, the head of the Maryland State Department of Education and the named defendant in the *Bradford* suit. At a state school board meeting, the students attempted to place her under citizens' arrest for failing to comply with Judge Kaplan's orders. At the next school board meeting, students performed a "die-in" outside the building. Inspired by antitobacco commercials, some students read devastating statistics about Baltimore schools and incarceration rates while others feigned death. Students noted that 52 percent of black men in Baltimore aged twenty to thirty were in prison or jail, on probation, or on parole.[26] An *Education Week* study found that only 38.5 percent of Baltimore students graduated high school in four years, the second lowest rate in the country.[27] The contrast between school and jail has become a symbolic part of all of the group's campaigns and shaped the group's signature phrase: "No Education! No Life!"

The students proceeded to organize a march in February 2005, followed by a student strike with students from twenty-eight schools.

Meanwhile, thirteen BAP members attended Moses's national meeting, Quality Education as a Civil Right, with academics, organizers, and young people from across the country. They returned to Baltimore with a much clearer idea of what a quality education could look like and a greater determination to press their cause.

In May 2005, on the fifty-first anniversary of the decision in *Brown* v. *Board of Education of Topeka, Kansas*, the students held a rally at the Inner Harbor in Baltimore, marched to the state board's office, and attempted civil disobedience. The students put up "Wanted" posters for Grasmick, Governor Robert Ehrlich, and Mayor Martin O'Malley on the Nancy S. Grasmick Building.

From demanding money to demanding quality education

A new crisis hit Baltimore schools in the 2005–2006 school year. In response to a state mandate citing underuse of space, the Baltimore City Board of School Commissioners voted to close 15 percent of the district's school space. BAP students were able to use this threat to organize youth on a broader scale. With help from the Baltimore Education Advocates, BAP students came up with "the ABC plan." They argued that schools should not be closed until basic school needs were met: **A**rt, music, physical, and computer education in every school; **B**uildings repaired and renovated; and **C**lass size at a maximum of twenty students. In this way, the students were able to continue to fight for $800 million in state funds and link their efforts to a demand for a quality education.

In order to get a broader base of youth to the planning table, BAP students organized a series of Saturday conferences. At these meetings, over two hundred students brainstormed ways to effect change. The conferences always ended with poetry, rap, and music. As BAP student Charnell Covert explains, "The spoken word and hip-hop is a way to broaden the work to a wider youth community, a way to celebrate ourselves and our culture, and expand the culture of activism."

BAP proved able to lead a three-day student strike with over nine hundred participants in March 2006. BAP students declared the fall of 2006 "Freedom Fall," calling it "Baltimore City's version of Mississippi's 1964 Freedom Summer." The students organized the election of a Maryland Freedom Board of Education, in explicit homage to the Mississippi Freedom Democratic Party.

The Freedom Fall campaign gained more publicity for the group's cause, and BAP's organizing continues. However, despite its impressive work, the group has struggled to achieve its ultimate goals. The state has not paid the court-ordered funds to Baltimore or moved in any other way to accelerate funding to the starved Baltimore school system. Moreover, several Baltimore schools were closed in 2006. Nevertheless, BAP counts as victories increased attendance at mass rallies, greater media coverage, a more educated public, a wider base of active students, and acknowledgment from power elites. In addition, it has received some national recognition for its efforts, as students presented their work at a National Congressional Black Caucus meeting and elsewhere.

In BAP students' own view, perhaps the group's most significant accomplishment has been to find a compelling way to make Bob Moses's idea of putting themselves central to society a reality. One of the powerful aspects of youth organizing for school reform is that education is such a defining aspect of youth life. BAP has shown that organizing for school reform can be a way to get youth to feel central to school (that is, society) and act that way. As BAP student Chris Goodman notes, "A key element is education, because I don't think enough people know that people have the power, not the politicians. Then people would understand what they need to do to help make change."[28]

Conclusion

The HSTF and BAP cases demonstrate the growing potential for youth organizing to become a force for school reform in our nation's cities. They illustrate how students can reverse the deficit paradigm to act out of their own self-interest to become agents of change. Although both cases show how self-interest provides a basis for engaging in school reform, they also demonstrate that understandings of self-interest can grow and develop through participation in organizing efforts. BAP started organizing in response to the threat of a budget cut to its tutoring program. But as they began to organize, BAP leaders grew to expand their sense of self-interest to encompass a quality education for all students in Baltimore. Meanwhile, HSTF organized first to get a community center in its neighborhood. Women in the project then began to raise concerns about their experience with sexual harassment. Through the relationships they built by working together, young women and men were able to come to a shared understanding of their interest in healthy relationships for all young people.

Our two cases show some of the different ways that youth organizing can engage in school reform work. The BAP focuses on increasing finances to underresourced schools and more recently has added its ABC program for improved schooling and a quality education. The HSTF focuses on issues of climate and relationships in schools. Other groups across the country have engaged in a variety of types of campaigns to open small high schools, improve teacher-student relationships, and gain access to college preparatory curricula, among other issues.[29] More research will be needed to compare the experiences of different approaches to school reform and to better assess the ability of youth organizing groups to achieve their goals.

The cases also illustrate the shift in the youth organizing field from a focus on youth development and community issues toward school reform action. Several reasons suggest themselves for this shift. Community-oriented youth organizing in the 1990s began at least in part as a response to the perceived crisis in urban communities: the rise of drugs, violence, and crime.[30] By the late 1990s, young people faced mounting attention to a perceived crisis in urban schooling and a series of government initiatives to reform schools, from testing requirements to efforts at privatization. Youth organizing around education reform began at least partly in response to this heightened attention to school failure.[31] BAP's focus on math literacy and college access as the new issues of a civil rights movement illustrates a growing understanding of the relationship between education and racial justice.

Youth organizing groups have begun to show how to create a base of student participation through organizing efforts. Both HSTF and BAP built a base first at the neighborhood level or in programming, which they then leveraged into school reform. This prior work helped create a core group of leaders and built legitimacy and recognition for the group's ability to effect change among city elites. The experience of both groups suggests the need for a base of participation and power as a prerequisite for entering the difficult terrain of education politics. Historically young people have played important roles in social movements in both the United States and internationally. Young people led lunch counter sit-ins in the civil rights movement, and schoolchildren led marches and protests in the antiapartheid movement in South Africa. Participation in these movements certainly provided an important learning and developmental opportunity for young people, sometimes profoundly shaping the course of their lives. But young people also constituted a powerful force for change in those movements. Today youth organizing continues to offer a vehicle for positive youth development and social change in communities. It has also become a new force in school reform for the benefit of those who have the greatest interest and desire for a high-quality education.

Notes

1. Ginwright, S. (2003). *Youth organizing: Expanding possibilities for youth development.* New York: Funders Collaborative on Youth Organizing; Checkoway, B., Richards-Schuster, K., Abdullah, S., Aragon, M., Facio, E., Figueroa, L., et al. (2003). Young people as competent citizens. *Community Development Journal, 38*(4), 298–309.

2. Checkoway, B., & Richards-Schuster, K. (2006). Youth participation for educational reform in low-income communities of color. In S. Ginwright, P. Noguera, & J. Cammarota (Eds.), *Beyond resistance: Youth activism and community change* (pp. 319–332). New York: Routledge; Mediratta, K. (2006). A rising movement. *National Civic Review, 95*(1), 15–22.

3. Cahill, M. (1997). *Youth development and community development: Promises and challenges of convergence.* Takoma Park, MD: Forum for Youth Investment; Ginwright, S., & James, T. (2002). From assets to agents of change: Social justice, organizing, and youth development. In B. Kirshner, J. L. O'Donoghue, & M. McLaughlin (Eds.), *Youth participation: Improving institutions and communities* (pp. 27–46). New Directions for Youth Development, no. 96. San Francisco: Jossey-Bass.

4. Endo, T. (2002). *Youth engagement in community-driven school reform.* Oakland, CA: Social Policy Research Associates.

5. Alcala, C. (2005). *6–1 victory for Los Angeles Unified students.* Retrieved May 10, 2007, from http://innercitystruggle.org/story.php?story=131.

6. Californians for Justice Education Fund. (2004). *The ABC's of justice: Students and parents fighting for racial justice in California schools.* Oakland, CA: Californians for Justice.

7. Ginwright, S. (2003). *Youth organizing: Expanding possibilities for youth development.* New York: Funders Collaborative on Youth Organizing. P. 2.

8. Fisher, R. (1994). *Let the people decide: Neighborhood organizing in America* (Updated ed.). New York: Twayne.

9. Carson, C. (1981). *In struggle: SNCC and the black awakening of the 1960s.* Cambridge, MA: Harvard University Press; Muñoz Jr., C. (1989). *Youth, identity, power: The Chicano movement.* New York: Verso.

10. Robnett, B. (1997). *How long? How long? African-American women in the struggle for civil rights.* New York: Oxford University Press.

11. Ginwright. (2003).

12. Mohamed, I., & Wheeler, W. (2001). *Broadening the bounds of youth development: Youth as engaged citizens.* Takoma Park, MD: Innovation Center for Community and Youth Development.

13. Ginwright and James. (2002); Watts, R. J., Williams, N. C., & Jagers, R. J. (2003). Sociopolitical development. *American Journal of Community Psychology, 31*(1/2), 185–194.

14. Checkoway & Richards-Schuster. (2006); Mediratta. (2006).

15. Blackburn, B. R. (2005). *Classroom motivation from A to Z: How to engage your students in learning.* Larchmont, NY: Eye on Education; Perry, T. (2003). Up from the parched earth: Toward a theory of African-American achievement. In T. Perry, C. Steele, & A. Hilliard III (Eds.), *Young, gifted and black: Promoting high achievement among African-American students.* Boston: Beacon Press.

16. Haste, H. (2004). Constructing the citizen. *Political Psychology, 25*(3), 413–436; Perry. (2003).

17. Warren, M. R. (2005). Communities and schools: A new view of urban education reform. *Harvard Educational Review, 75*(2), 133–173.

18. Alinsky, S. D. (1971). *Rules for radicals: A practical primer for realistic radicals.* New York: Random House.

19. Hyde Square Task Force. (2007). *About us.* Retrieved May 7, 2007, from www.hydesquare.org.

20. Van Delft, P. (2006, June 8). The A, B, Cs of sexual harassment: Local students unite against lessons no one needs. *The Second: A Weekly Guide to Life in the City,* p. 3.

21. Miller, Y. (2006, June 1–7). Survey: Students face sexual harassment in HS. *Metro: Boston Globe Media,* p. 3.

22. "Working the Demand Side of the Equation" comes from Bob Moses at a session of the Congressional Black Caucus, September 23, 2005, as recorded by Thomas Nikundiwe.

23. Moses, R. P., & Cobb Jr., C. E. (2001). *Radical equations: Math literacy and civil rights.* Boston: Beacon Press.

24. Moses & Cobb. (2001).
25. *Bradford et al.* v. *Maryland State Board of Education et al.*, 94340058/CE 189672 (1994).
26. Ziedenberg, J., & Lotke, E. (2005). *Tipping point: Maryland's overuse of incarceration and the impact on community safety.* Washington, DC: Justice Policy Institute.
27. Neufeld, S. (2006, June 27). Schools challenge report. *Baltimore Sun.*
28. Torres, J. (2006, November 22). After-coup special. *Baltimore City Paper.*
29. Alcala. (2005); Mediratta & Shah, this volume.
30. HoSand, D. (2003). *Youth and community organizing today.* New York: Funders Collaborative on Youth Organizing.
31. Mediratta. (2006).

MARK R. WARREN *is associate professor in the Graduate School of Education at Harvard University.*

MEREDITH MIRA *is a doctoral student at the Harvard Graduate School of Education.*

THOMAS NIKUNDIWE *is a doctoral student at the Harvard Graduate School of Education.*

Despite resistance from some educators and differences in the cultures of schools and organizing groups, young people are negotiating reform to win important changes in schooling practices and policies.

3

Negotiating reform: Young people's leadership in the educational arena

Seema Shah, Kavitha Mediratta

IN SPRING 2004, a Philadelphia high school with a history of poor academic performance defied the odds to become one of three comprehensive high schools in the city to meet adequate yearly progress standards (AYP) on the state standardized exams.

The school's success drew accolades until students affiliated with Youth United for Change (YUC), a local youth organizing group, raised questions about how the school had reached AYP. Students reported serious concerns about test-taking practices—teachers completing blank answers for students, tests administered with instructional aids on the walls—and the pervasive practice of pulling students from core subject courses for intensive test preparation.

Youth United for Change students led a two-year campaign to improve test-taking practices at the school. Students surveyed peers about their experiences with testing, produced a report documenting concerns and recommendations for improvement, held individual meetings with district administrators to express their concerns, and presented testimony to the Philadelphia School Reform Commission.[1] Although a district investigation found no

NEW DIRECTIONS FOR YOUTH DEVELOPMENT, NO. 117, SPRING 2008 © WILEY PERIODICALS, INC.
Published online in Wiley InterScience (www.interscience.wiley.com) • DOI: 10.1002/yd.246

evidence of wrongdoing, when additional test monitors were placed at the school the following year, test scores plummeted by 23 percent, and the school failed to meet AYP.[2]

The campaign ultimately resulted in the adoption of a new set of district-wide standards. In its press release, the Philadelphia School District noted that "incorporating suggestions from YUC, the District is updating [its standardized testing] practices"—among them, posting testing procedures in all schools and limiting specific test preparation classes to elective or noninstructional hours.[3]

Shortly after YUC convened a joint press conference with the district to announce the new testing practices, YUC youth leaders began to experience what they viewed as retaliation by their school's administration. Seniors who had participated in the campaign were not allowed to go on a class trip, even though all of them were on the honor roll. In addition, the principal rejected YUC's request to conduct outreach during lunch, as other school clubs do, arguing that the organizing group's membership drive would disrupt the school day. Summing up the school's response, one student said, "They hate us, they fear us. They're scared."

One year later, YUC organizers continue to be restricted from holding student meetings on school property. Students now travel forty-five minutes weekly to meet at the YUC office.

The YUC story highlights how high school students' campaigns for school reform can catalyze important changes in schooling practices and policies—changes that ultimately promote increased accountability to provide a quality education, particularly to students of color, who are poorly served by urban education systems. But the resistance to student activism underscores the tensions that can arise between students and school officials when students wage campaigns focused on educational improvement.

This article examines young people's experiences as they organize to expand educational opportunities in urban school districts. We report findings from a Mott Foundation–funded six-year study of the education organizing of three youth organizations: Sistas and Brothas United of the Northwest Bronx Community and Clergy Coalition in Bronx, New York; South Central Youth Empowered

Thru Action of the Community Coalition for Substance Abuse
Prevention and Treatment in Los Angeles; and Youth United for
Change in Philadelphia. Drawing on more than eighty interviews
with students, organizers, and school, district, and municipal
administrators, we examine the impact of youth-led improvement
efforts and assess how young people are negotiating the dynamics
of race and class, as well as the cultural norms of educational
bureaucracies, to improve schooling outcomes.

Youth organizing and its impact on schools and districts

High school students have a long history of activism on education
issues; examples include youth-led mobilizations during the 1968
Chicano walkouts in East Los Angeles and the school desegregation
battles in Philadelphia. What has changed is the exponential growth
of youth organizing within the institutional context of community-
based organizations. Indeed, youth organizing groups focused on
education reform are expanding so rapidly that it is difficult to assess
the exact number of groups in existence. A 2002 report identified at
least forty such groups in the San Francisco Bay Area alone and suggested that many more are active nationally.[4]

The youth organizing groups in our study seek to systematically
develop leadership and build power among young people. To this
end, not only do these groups work with young people to develop
a structural analysis of the disparities in educational, economic, and
social provision and outcomes, but they also actively engage youth
in social change efforts to alter these conditions. In addition, groups
provide students with academic support, including tutoring, home-
work help, and college access activities.

These youth-led organizing efforts are influencing educational
decision making in significant ways. Youth groups have pushed for
greater schooling accountability for educational outcomes,
expanded student voice in schooling decisions, and increased access
to culturally relevant and academically rigorous curricula.[5] Indeed,
despite the tensions that youth organizing elicits, the district and

municipal leaders we interviewed credited youth organizations with significant roles in identifying schooling problems and building political and public support for the necessary policy shifts and resource investments.

At the district-level, both Sistas and Brothas United (SBU) and South Central Youth Empowered Thru Action (SC-YEA) have been credited with securing funds for facilities improvements. More recently, SC-YEA's district-wide organizing has focused on expanding college access. Its efforts, in collaboration with a citywide coalition of community organizations, resulted in the passage of a June 2005 school board resolution mandating college preparatory curricula in all district high schools. YUC's organizing has not only resulted in a new set of district test preparation standards and practices, but has also begun to transform high school education in Philadelphia through a district-wide strategy of creating small schools.

Youth organizing groups have also made significant inroads at the school level. One notable example is the creation of the Leadership Institute, a school focused on social justice that SBU opened in the Bronx. Youth led the campaign to win approval for the school and participated in developing the curriculum, recruiting students, selecting the principal, and hiring staff.

Although implementation of these victories is highly variable—indeed, in all three cities, youth are struggling to hold educators accountable to agreed-on reforms—what is clear is that youth organizing efforts are prodding districts and schools toward greater equity in access to quality education.

How educators position themselves in relation to youth organizing

Our research found that educators respond to youth organizing groups' campaigns for school improvement in a variety of ways, across a continuum of supportiveness to defensiveness (Figure 3.1). Supportive educators understood that organizing involves mobilizing student voice to pressure schools and districts to change through

Figure 3.1. Continuum of supportive and defensive behaviors

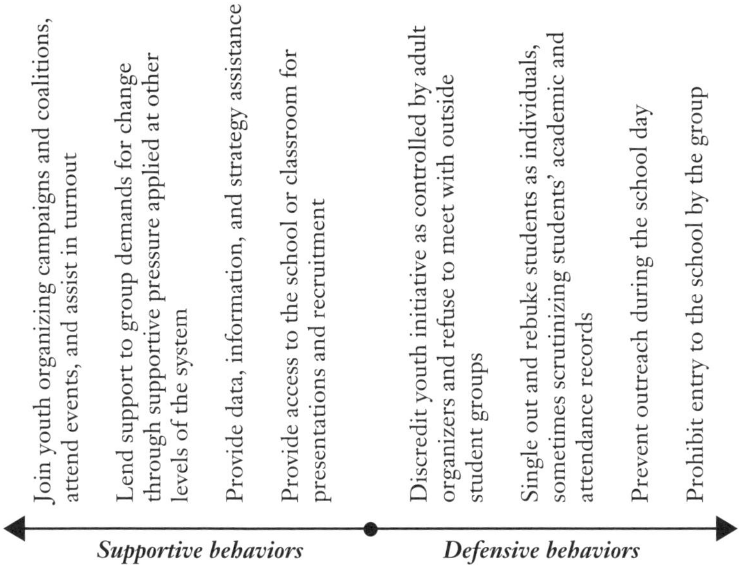

a variety of relational and confrontational tactics. These educators also understood that participation from all students across race, class, or academic performance, rather than the participation of only elite or good students, is necessary for meaningful change to occur. Because of such understanding, these educators acted as critical allies in supporting youth-generated school reform agendas. An organizer describes his group's relationship with one district administrator: "She tells us what to do, what not to do, and she gets it. One, she gets what we're doing, and two, she's not threatened by it . . . so she's really about giving out guidance on avoiding mine-fields. . . . At the end of the day, she's going to have our back."

Educators who were not vocal advocates of the groups nonetheless were supportive by not getting in the way of students' efforts—providing access to the school, allowing students to make classroom presentations about their organization and its campaigns, and coordinating logistical support such as reserving classroom space for meetings.

NEW DIRECTIONS FOR YOUTH DEVELOPMENT • DOI: 10.1002/yd

Yet students at all three sites also noted defensive postures that their critiques of schooling conditions elicited from school-level staff, even when their organizing was not targeted directly at the school. A student in Los Angeles reflects, "We had principals that were mad at us because we pointed out how poor the conditions were in their schools. They took it personally, as opposed to feeding us information off the record so we could bring pressure to bear to help them."

As we showed at the start of this article, some educators responded defensively by limiting groups' access to the school, taking punitive measures against students involved in organizing efforts, and discrediting the work of youth organizing groups.

Dynamics between educators and youth

Most educators are generally only peripherally engaged in youth organizing efforts, rather than being supportive or defensive, and consequently they do not understand the nature of the work. Indeed, much of our analysis of school-level interactions comes from interviews with youth and organizers, because few educators were connected deeply enough to youth organizing groups to comment thoughtfully on the processes and impacts of their organizing.

Time demands on school officials, as well as leadership and staff turnover within both schools and youth organizations, contribute to the difficulty of building deep, long-term relationships between the two constituencies. Yet our interviews also suggest that interactions between students and educators are shaped by low expectations for urban students of color. Moreover, radically different cultural norms and assumptions differentiate schools from youth organizations.

Race- and class-based assumptions about student leadership

The students and organizers we interviewed believe that educators' responses to their demands for reform are defined by deeply entrenched class- and race-based assumptions about student capacities. Importantly, all three youth organizations in our study serve students attending underresourced schools in predominantly poor African American and Latino neighborhoods. At the core of each youth group's philosophy is the belief that all students have the potential to attend college, a conviction that students and organizers assert is not widely shared by educators in their schools.

In Los Angeles, for example, when SC-YEA pushed for greater access to college preparatory curriculum, it encountered resistance from some teachers, school board members, and legislators, who argued that mandating a more rigorous curriculum would not only increase the dropout rate but also reduce the labor pool for low-wage jobs.[6] A high school student recounts her testimony before the state legislature, where she spoke in favor of a mandatory college preparatory curriculum for the district:

I remember after I did my speech, the [legislator] who was against it started speaking and then I remember him making a comment about what's gonna happen when [his] car breaks down, who's gonna fix [his] car, and I really felt like . . . he was saying that because he thought that's where we belonged. We belong working for them, fixing their cars, doing their hair, stuff like that. I really felt hurt, because I felt that it's not for him to make that decision; it's for the students to make that decision.

Students reported several instances of adult skepticism about their proposals, which they believe stems from low expectations of their potential, not only as students but also as contributors to solving schooling problems. At one Los Angeles high school, a plan for integrating student feedback into teacher evaluations elicited disbelief. An organizer recalls, "[At the] follow-up meeting with our organizer . . . [one of the teachers said] there was no way the students would have come up with that, that this was a college-level analysis [and our] students don't have the capacity to come up with a policy like that."

Similarly, organizers recounted incidents where school-level educators questioned the legitimacy of student demands for school improvement when their own academic performance was less than stellar. An organizer explains, "There have been times where . . . [students] get pulled into the principal's office. And they say, how can you demand college prep classes when you're failing this class?" As one administrator made clear, despite the practical benefits of engaging with students of all academic backgrounds, few educators actually do so. A district official in New York explains:

The kids that get voice are the kids that can get all A's and B's and come to school every day—precisely the kind of kids that get the job done, but you really need to engage the others. . . . When kids are saying to you explicitly, "We don't like this about our schools, we have poor teachers, we have poor administration, we have this . . . ," people aren't comfortable with that, [but] if you exclude kids' voice, you end up with lots of bad problems.

In most schools, student leadership is conceptualized as participation in student government and extracurricular clubs, in which access is often limited to students who stay out of trouble and perform well in school.[7] District vehicles for student voice tend to operate within the same paradigm. To the extent that educators are accustomed to hearing from student voices, they hear from a minority of academically and socially successful students, who also tend to be the most socioeconomically advantaged. Youth we interviewed who are active in their school's student government noted the tendency of these school-sanctioned leadership bodies to be far less inclusive than their organizing counterparts.

Cultural differences between educational bureaucracies and youth organizing groups

Clearly race and class dynamics are a dominant force in defining how adults respond to young people's leadership. In addition, our data suggest that differences in the norms of schools and youth organizations—top-down and often bureaucratically rigid institutions versus bottom-up and more fluid grassroots organizations—also mediate the possibilities for young people's education reform leadership.

Youth groups typically work through participatory and iterative cycles of defining a problem, researching and building consensus on proposals for reform ("demands"), and identifying decision makers ("targets") who have the authority to grant their demands.

Negotiation occurs in large group settings, led by a young person, who follows an agenda aimed at securing a clear statement of support from targets. In contrast, decision making in schools occurs through a well-defined chain of command in which the space for action is constrained by political pressures and by a complex web of rules, regulations, and relationships (Table 3.1).

These cultural differences make educators uneasy about building alliances with organizations that they know little about and do not control. School officials worry that outside groups do not sufficiently appreciate the complexity of issues within the school. As a result, school officials believe that an outside organization will inject chaos into an already challenging environment. A district administrator explains:

You can't just have anybody coming into your school, riling up students without a track record and sense of mutual accountability. I think we are accountable to community organizations, but they are also accountable to us—because they are not there every day—accountable for the safety of those children. And they don't always know the work that a school is trying to do, and maybe organizations will just come in without regard for the good work, in spite of the difficulties, [taking place] in schools.

Cultural differences between youth organizing groups and school and district bureaucracies also shape the possibilities for

Table 3.1. Cultural differences between schools and youth organizations

	Schools	*Youth Groups*
Culture	Hierarchical, compliance orientation	Democratic, problem-solving orientation
Decision making	Top-down chain of command; decisions made by administrators	Participatory and inclusive; decisions made by the group, generally by consensus
Locus of expertise	School leaders and professional leaders are experts	Participants: everyone has something to contribute
External pressures	Political interests and regulatory constraints	Need to deliver concrete victories to constituents on concerns

NEW DIRECTIONS FOR YOUTH DEVELOPMENT • DOI: 10.1002/yd

negotiation sessions. As adults, educational decision makers are more experienced meeting goers and more adept at educational and bureaucratic language. In response, youth groups tend to use a disciplined format for meetings, emphasizing the need to stick to the agenda and pressing for clearly defined answers to their questions, to prevent educators from shifting attention away from the issues the young people are raising. Youth organizations use this approach strategically to level the playing field between young people and educational decision makers. But as educators point out, this approach can make it difficult to engage in dialogue and identify acceptable compromises. According to a Philadelphia district official, "I think as they ask for adults to listen to them. I think sometimes they might do a better job of listening to adults. And I see in many cases [the group] has a firm agenda and generally doesn't vary from that agenda presented. And I think the same adaptation and flexibility that they request, when it's modeled on their end, I think we're gonna make progress."

Youth and adult negotiations also carry an inherent tension between young people wanting to engage educators as equal partners and yet needing adults to be powerful, perhaps more than they actually are. Indeed, several administrators noted the disconnect between young people's insistence on immediate action to alter schooling conditions and the political, financial, and time constraints that administrators face, all of which limit their ability to meet external demands for change. A Philadelphia district administrator observes:

At times . . . [the group doesn't] give a damn about protocol, [does]n't care about the chain of command. They will backdoor you in a minute if they think you are blowing them off. And you know what? If you're blowing them off, you deserve it. But if you're not and you're really limited and you can't, a heads-up would be nice, for them to say, "You know what, I'm taking it here." That would be nice. . . . I will say that some of it I think is born out of lack of trust toward the institution. What we need to learn as a big bad institution is not to take things personally. And I think that is one of the things [the group] might say. . . . "You know what? This isn't about [an administrator], this is about [our] education."

Negotiating reform

To move their school reform agendas forward, youth must develop ways to overcome the obstacles described in the previous section—in particular, educators' low expectations for young people's capacity to engage in education reform, as well as differences in the cultural norms of schools and youth organizations that exacerbate feelings of vulnerability, pressure, and defensiveness among educators. Youth organizing groups are responding to these challenges through intensive political education and issue analysis and targeted relationship building with education stakeholders, including district administrators, around mutual goals and self interest.

Political education and issue analysis

Youth organizing groups devote considerable time orienting youth to key players within their local districts, with an emphasis on understanding who possesses decision-making authority and the implications of changing educational policies. The youth we interviewed understood the political landscape of their local school systems, easily referencing school board members and district officials in their conversation, as well as the key educational policy issues facing their district. In a survey of 124 youth leaders representing the three organizations in our study, 85 percent of youth reported that because of their involvement in the organizing group, they had become more knowledgeable about who makes the decisions about school and district policies, and 88 percent of youth reported that their involvement in organizing groups improved their knowledge of school policies.

In addition to sharpening the policy analysis skills of youth, organizing groups help their members develop structural critiques of school conditions. An organizer in Los Angeles describes the impact of SC-YEA's training curriculum:

Before [our training], when you ask our youth about what some of the main problems are and what to do to change them, their main solution a lot of times is we just need to get rid of teachers, get new teachers and we've got to get rid of the principals, because this one is problematic. After the [training], they understand that the issue is systemic. . . . The principal may be a part of it, but it's a much larger issue. And you have to get to the root of it and begin to talk about school culture, the curriculum, [and] the training that teachers get . . .

Organizers also support youth as they conduct their own research on education issues, often by surveying their fellow students about school resources and conditions. For instance, SC-YEA youth began their campaign for greater access to a college preparatory curriculum by analyzing the courses offered in their high schools, compiling data showing that their schools offered more courses in cosmetology and floor covering than math and science. Such research capacity, combined with training in public speaking, meeting facilitation, and negotiation skills, helps youth present their ideas in ways that demonstrate their knowledge and competence and begins to counter adult skepticism. As young people gain confidence, they are willing to confront adults on issues they care about. A student from Los Angeles explains, "We don't think we're above everybody, we don't think we know everything, we just think that we know certain stuff and we're not going to let it pass."

A New York City district administrator notes the impact of such intensive leadership development:

I tell you, [SBU youth leaders] come up here and have conversations with me . . . [and] one of the things that I find I can measure is . . . the *way* that they have conversations with me. I mean, if the kids can sit at a table, have a conversation with me around, this is the research I've done, this is the outcome, and this is where we want to go—I mean, that doesn't come out of the sky. . . . [SBU has] organized the kids to be good thinkers and to be able to speak to adults and not be afraid to speak to adults.

The extent to which information on schools and school improvement strategies is integrated into youth organizations' trainings has increased over time. In part, this evolution corresponds with the maturation of youth organizing for school reform nationally and a resulting dialogue about failures and effective strategies. Yet at the local level, most groups continue to struggle to gain access to rel-

evant information on school policies and performance and to bring
that information effectively into youth-led campaigns.

*Targeted relationship building with education stakeholders and
district administrators*

As part of mapping the school system's political landscape, organizers help youth assess political dynamics within their communities and build relationships to leverage support for their demands.
All three sites are actively involved in alliance-building efforts with
a broad cross-section of civic stakeholders to build collective
power and increase the pressure on decision makers to grant
youths' demands.

The extent of alliance building among youth organizations is
notable, particularly in the intensity and longevity of emerging relationships. At all three sites, youth organizations are working with
other groups to build a shared vision of reform across schools,
neighborhoods, and ethnic communities. In Philadelphia, for example, YUC joined with the Philadelphia Student Union to define and
advocate for a citywide high school equity agenda. In Los Angeles,
SC-YEA partnered with Inner City Struggle to define and fight for
a comprehensive college preparatory agenda. In New York City,
SBU worked with three youth organizations to form the citywide
Urban Youth Collaborative. By expanding the geographical base
and diversity of campaigns, such alliances help groups demonstrate
the systemic relevance and imperative of their demands.

In addition, all three youth organizations have collaborated with
education reform and research organizations to obtain information
on school reform initiatives, data on schooling conditions, and
assistance in designing, implementing, and analyzing student-led
research. For example, YUC youth worked with Research for
Action to conduct action research on student-teacher relationships
in new small schools.[8] In Los Angeles, the Institute for Democracy,
Education and Access at the University of California, Los Angeles,
and the Education Trust West provided crucial analyses in support
of SC-YEA's college preparatory curriculum campaign. And in New

York City, data analyses and research by the Annenberg Institute for School Reform helped inform SBU's school facilities, school safety, and college counseling campaigns.

In the best-case scenarios, strategic alliance building has enabled youth organizations to build relationships with district administrators and enlist them as critical allies in campaigns. An organizer in Los Angeles explains that such "inside-outside" strategies are crucial because "we know from past efforts that if we don't create the internal dialogue and if it's just strictly from the outside, [the reform's] gonna be resisted and it's not gonna be effective."

Because all three organizations in our study are either components of or affiliated with a longstanding adult-led community organization, they also draw on the organizational infrastructure and the political relationships developed by community residents and public school parents to buttress youth-led efforts. Interviewees recounted several instances where long-term organizational relationships were leveraged to counter resistance from school level educators. A student in Los Angeles offers this example:

The principals that we have now, well at first, they were really giving us the runaround. . . . We were trying to get on campus and when we'd show up, what I like to call their "goon" at the door, the security guard, just wouldn't let us in, [saying,] "Oh, you need to set up a meeting." And we tried to set up meetings and all that, and finally we contacted a superintendent, and I understand Community Coalition has a really strong relationship with her, and so immediately, we were let on campus.

Implications for education reform

A myriad of educational and social policies marginalize young people, particularly youth of color, in our schools and society. Even well-intentioned interventions inadvertently fix responsibility for poor outcomes on youth themselves rather than targeting the structural flaws within the systems that are designed to serve them.

Ginwright and James argue that organizing provides an avenue for young people to become "agents of change"—to confront individual-level analyses with demands for the systemic reforms necessary to end patterns of inequity in their communities.[9] As our research suggests, youth organizing groups are demonstrating notable successes in these efforts. Moreover, as district and municipal leaders point out, despite the tensions that erupt when young people organize in schools, their work contributes to reform in vital ways.

Importantly, youth organizing represents a different brand of youth voice—one that focuses on problem solving through a disciplined methodology of data collection, analysis, action, and reflection and represents a more diverse cross-section of youth than those traditionally engaged in school-provided structures. Because youth organizing groups tap into a broader cross-section of youth, these high school students often possess important knowledge about problems in schools that district leaders may not have previously known about. A superintendent notes the role that youth groups play in providing intelligence about the school system: "You know, bureaucracies have a tendency to try to limit the flow of bad news and increase the flow of good news. . . . And so I need access. I need to get information through nontraditional ways. And these groups, along with the teachers' union and the principals' association, provide me with that access."

In addition to identifying problems, youth organizations propose solutions that are informed by their own experiences. Indeed, the very direct nature of young people's experience of schooling problems can lead them to strategies that educators may not have considered. Administrators in New York City, for example, praised SBU for drawing attention to the worsening conditions of a large high school where the creation of new small schools had exacerbated overcrowding and increased the number of school safety incidents. SBU proposed creating a campus-based Student Success Center as a way to expand college preparatory supports while providing a space for students to get help in resolving issues before conflicts escalated into full-blown school safety incidents.[10]

Our interviews make clear that educators have much to gain from recognizing youth as critical stakeholders in school reform. Our data also suggest that both educators and youth organizing groups need to invest more energy in understanding each other's work and building more effective relationships. As youth organizing groups develop relationships with educators and negotiate their demands, they must acknowledge and account for the pressures imposed by educational bureaucracies if they want to expand their potential impact. Educators, for their part, need to create more inclusive spaces for youth leadership and understand the methods and goals of youth organizing groups. A senior district administrator and former principal in Philadelphia notes that the benefits of forging connections with youth organizing groups are mutual: "[At] the end of the day, we want the same thing: the best learning opportunities for our kids, to challenge them, to push them, to test them—not only academically, but socially. We want to graduate kids who believe in service. We want to graduate kids who have a moral approach and a moral compass. It may not always be pointing north, but you want kids who are reflective and I think these folks really try hard to get that going."

Notes

1. Youth United for Change. *Report on standardized testing and plan for improvement.* Unpublished manuscript. (2005).
2. Pennsylvania Department of Education. AYP results. [Electronic version]. http://www.pde.state.pa.us/a_and_t/lib/a_and_t/School_AYP_Status_2003-2006.pdf—125.0KB.
3. Philadelphia School District Office of Communications. (2006, January 12). *School district of Philadelphia, youth united for change unveil updates to standardized testing practices.* [Electronic version]. http://www.phila.k12.pa.us/offices/communications/press_releases/2006/01/17/youth_united.html.
4. Cervone, B. (2002). *Taking democracy in hand: Youth action for educational change in the San Francisco Bay Area.* Providence, RI: What Kids Can Do with the Forum for Youth Investment.
5. Mediratta, K. (2004). *Constituents of change.* New York: Institute for Education and Social Policy.
6. Hayasaki, E. (2005, May 29). Teachers give college prep plan an F. *Los Angeles Times,* B1.
7. Mediratta, K., Cohen, A., & Shah, S. (2007). Leveraging reform: Youth power in a smart education system. In R. Rothman (Ed.), *City schools: How districts and communities can create smart education systems* (pp. 99–116). Cambridge, MA: Harvard Educational Press.
8. Crosby, W., George, A., Hatch, A., Robinson, R., & Thomas, T. (2006). *Building respectful communities: Kensington students examine adult-student rela-*

tionships in their new small schools. Writing to be heard series. Philadelphia: Research for Action.

9. Ginwright, S., & James, T. (2002). From assets to agents of change: Social justice, organizing, and youth development. In B. Kirshner, J. L. O'Donoghue, & M. W. McLaughlin (Eds.), *Youth participation: Improving institutions and communities* (pp. 27–46). New Directions for Youth Development, no. 96. San Francisco: Jossey-Bass.

10. The Student Success Center concept was drawn from the work of the Philadelphia Student Union.

SEEMA SHAH *is a research associate at the Annenberg Institute for School Reform at Brown University.*

KAVITHA MEDIRATTA *is a principal associate at the Annenberg Institute for School Reform at Brown University.*

The executive director of a highly respected child advocacy organization reflects on her organization's history and why it has recently adopted more bottom-up community organizing strategies.

4

Thirty years of advocacy in San Francisco: Lessons learned and the next generation of leadership

NTanya Lee

COLEMAN ADVOCATES FOR Children and Youth is a thirty-year-old local child advocacy organization in San Francisco. Founded in the early years of the contemporary child advocacy movement, around the same time that the Children's Defense Fund began, Coleman Advocates is now recognized as a national leader in the field for its groundbreaking strategies that have won more than $100 million in safety net services to low-income children and families and created a powerful voice for a once-ignored constituency in local politics. With strong leadership and a very small staff, we have built a large and powerful political base of support for children's issues and a track record of independent, passionate, and effective work on behalf of children in San Francisco. Our accomplishments include creating a community-based system for previously incarcerated status offenders, establishing the nation's most extensive local system of child care subsidies and support, winning funding for a citywide network of school-based health centers, establishing policies that

NEW DIRECTIONS FOR YOUTH DEVELOPMENT, NO. 117, SPRING 2008 © WILEY PERIODICALS, INC.
Published online in Wiley InterScience (www.interscience.wiley.com) • DOI: 10.1002/yd.247

regulate school-based policing, and creating the voter-mandated Children's Amendment, which now funds more than $50 million a year in children's services in San Francisco.

Although the litany of Coleman's policy victories is impressive, it is the evolution of our strategies for change—our theoretical and practical approaches to achieving social change for the city's children and families—that are an especially compelling aspect of Coleman's story. This is particularly true at this moment in the history of nonprofit 501(c)(3) professional advocacy organizations in the United States. The children born in the 1960s have begun to take the reins of the organizations founded by the baby boomers and activists of the 1960s and 1970s. We are a new generation of U.S.-based leaders who know our history but have our eyes firmly on the horizon of seeming impossibility.

Almost three years ago, our executive director of twenty-six years, Margaret Brodkin, was appointed by Mayor Gavin Newsom to become the director of the city department that Coleman, through Brodkin's leadership, had helped to create and fund over the past three decades. With this appointment, the city gained a veteran child advocate to run the Department of Children, Youth and Their Families, and Coleman gained a close friend in city government—but it also needed a new executive director. After a carefully planned six-month transition period, I was named executive director, and the organization began an exciting period of self-reflection, evaluation, and change. We are now two years into Coleman's fourth major strategy shift, building on the remarkable successes and lessons learned from our first thirty years. In this article, I discuss my personal view of the evolution of our core strategies and theories of change.

―――――――――

Coleman, me, and the next generation

I am the first person of color to lead Coleman and one of a few in the nation to lead child advocacy organizations. Even in 2007, most advocacy organizations continue to be run by white leadership, even those whose constituencies are overwhelmingly people of

NEW DIRECTIONS FOR YOUTH DEVELOPMENT • DOI: 10.1002/yd

color.[1] I am not simply bringing a different racial identity to this role. Rather, I am bringing different legacies of leadership, different traditions of political thought and struggle, and a new vantage point from which to reflect on and rethink the past and present of the organization I have inherited.

Born in 1969, I am the child of black student activists of the late 1960s and came of age under Reaganomics. I am named after the child of an African liberation leader and discovered the work of Franz Fanon, June Jordan, Nikki Giovanni, and W.E.B. DuBois in my own house. Growing up between two households—one upper middle class and the other struggling to keep the heat on—I learned about the contradictions of the American dream through personal experience. I grew angry about the welfare system's hostility toward my mother's attempts to get a college education, about being the only black student in high school honors classes, and about politicians who cared more about funding military expansion than helping ordinary people raise children with dignity. I had strong feminist, multiracial, populist, progressive politics long before I knew the names for these things.

Over the past twenty-five years, I have seen radical, progressive, liberal, and conservative politics up close and have personally experienced a wide range of social change strategies and tactics. I became the organizational leader of Coleman Advocates at age thirty-five, after four years as Coleman's director of youth policy and youth organizing. I took the executive director job because it was a rare opportunity to continue an organization's extraordinary legacy of principled and effective work, and it was an opportunity to help build the next generation of leaders for social justice.

I am among a new generation of progressive leaders of color. We are the children of the 1960s who learned about social movements from history books and family conversation. We are the college-educated beneficiaries of the end of Jim Crow, of affirmative action and efforts to create equal opportunity for poor, working-class, and minority children. Our heroes and heroines fought for the self-determination of people of color all over the world, as well as the basic rights of citizenship under the U.S. Constitution. We look to the organizing tradition of Ella Baker and the Student Nonviolent

NEW DIRECTIONS FOR YOUTH DEVELOPMENT • DOI: 10.1002/yd

Coordinating Committee for inspiration more than to Martin Luther King's ministerial leadership of the Southern Christian Leadership Conference, and to Fannie Lou Hamer's Mississippi Freedom Democratic Party more than Lyndon Johnson's War on Poverty. And yet with our principled commitment to democratic participation and human rights, we have a pragmatism that might disappoint our heroes. Perhaps this is because the movements that shaped us have been under attack our entire lives. We are managers *and* dreamers, able to hold both traditional models of nonprofit administration and radical ideas about social justice simultaneously in our field of vision. We have experienced the power of multiracial alliances, understand the need to move beyond protest politics, and are building effective, powerful organizations that win concrete improvements for our communities in the short term as we keep our eyes on the prize of long-term transformative social change.

_____

Thirty years of strategies for change

As a member of this new generation, I look back at Coleman's thirty years and see three major strategy shifts. We are now in the midst of the fourth.

Coleman's early years could be characterized by a famous Margaret Mead quote: "A small group of thoughtful people can change the world. Indeed, it's the only thing that ever has." In our case, a three-year-old in an isolation cell in San Francisco's Juvenile Hall was the spark that led Coleman's courageous founder, Jean Jacobs, to begin a lifelong campaign to help children in the juvenile justice and foster care systems. Gertrude Coleman, impressed by Jacobs's resolve, left a small trust to the San Francisco Foundation, which created Coleman and appointed its first board of directors. Coleman began operations in 1975. Throughout the 1970s and early 1980s, with a professional advocacy staff of fewer than five, Coleman focused on reforming systems that served abused, neglected, and status offender children. Coleman's goal, which was accomplished, was to have ser-

NEW DIRECTIONS FOR YOUTH DEVELOPMENT • DOI: 10.1002/yd

vices for these children removed from the Juvenile Hall and have comprehensive family-focused services placed in the community. Both Jean Jacobs and Margaret Brodkin viewed themselves as activist social workers who refused to be "nice" and entered the political fray to fight for poor children whom no one else seemed to care about.

The assumptions and ideas behind Coleman's work in these first stages held much in common with the ideas of most child advocacy and antipoverty advocacy programs from that era:

• Though flawed, our economy and system of government are the best possible and work for most people. Poor children and families lack equal access to the opportunities this system provides, and new policies can make the system work better for all people.
• Children lack the right to vote; poor children and families lack political power and are at a disadvantage compared to more powerful interests in an otherwise basically fair democratic system. To address children's needs, professional advocates and engaged, outraged citizens must speak out on their behalf and develop a power base that can compete with other interests.
• Poor families, especially poor urban families of color, are not able or willing to effectively win change on their own behalf in the policymaking arena; professional advocates and experts must speak for them.
• As long as the majority of voters (and public officials) are white and middle class, race and class-neutral messages to win policy change for all children are more pragmatic, as they are more inclusive and do not alienate the political base needed to address children's needs.

By the mid-1980s, Coleman's predominant strategy of inside pressure by professional advocates was under question by Brodkin herself. Years of working mostly with the administrators of public systems, not the elected officials who had political power over them, had led to significant reforms, but opportunities for even broader impact and deeper system change seemed to be limited.

NEW DIRECTIONS FOR YOUTH DEVELOPMENT • DOI: 10.1002/yd

Coleman's entrance in the heated and high-visibility world of city budget politics in the late 1980s led to the second shift in strategy. We began to supplement our core inside advocacy approach with stronger outside pressure, including mobilizing hundreds of advocates for children to pressure city hall, educating voters about electoral candidates' position on children's issues and holding them accountable to campaign promises to children, and using the media more assertively to gain influence in the political arena. This strategy came to a peak in 1991 when Brodkin organized fifty thousand voters to sign petitions to put our landmark Children's Amendment on the ballot, and it passed despite the overwhelming lack of support from elected officials and political insiders. With this success, San Francisco became the first city in the country to guarantee funding each year for children, and advocates for children gained a new position of power in city politics.

Proposition J, as the new law became known, not only ushered in a new era for San Francisco but set a precedent for cities around the country. In 2000, with the Children's Amendment about to sunset, Coleman led the campaign to have it renewed. The Children's Amendment was reauthorized overwhelmingly by 74 percent of San Francisco voters in November 2000. The new and improved legislation increases the size of the Children's Fund, now almost $60 million a year, and extends it until 2016. More than forty thousand children now receive services annually through agencies funded with these dollars—almost half of the city's entire child population.[2]

As Coleman's work and influence broadened considerably, the next shift emerged. It became clear during the Proposition J campaign that young people were particularly compelling public spokespersons for children's policies, as they were assumed to have no political agenda. Under Brodkin's leadership, Youth Making a Change (Y-MAC) was launched in 1991 as Coleman's youth-led advocacy arm, giving scores of urban, low-income, working-class young people the opportunity to develop authentic leadership in moving their own youth agenda through city government. Based on Y-MAC's success, we launched Parent Advocates for Youth (PAY), which trained dozens of strong grassroots parent leaders, mostly women of color, to lead PAY campaigns to improve the

NEW DIRECTIONS FOR YOUTH DEVELOPMENT • DOI: 10.1002/yd

parks' recreation facilities, the schools, and the juvenile justice system. By the mid-1990s, Coleman was a unique hybrid of professionally driven and constituency-led advocacy.

New leadership faces the new San Francisco

I came into the executive director role at a critical time in San Francisco history. The 2000 census revealed that the city now had the smallest percentage of children of any city in the United States. Decades of intensifying gentrification, escalating housing prices, increasing income inequality, and profound shifts in domestic and international migration trends had conspired to permanently reshape the landscape, culture, and politics of our city. Working-class and middle-income families were increasingly forced out of the city simply to make ends meet. Declining school enrollment forced the city to close schools while luxury condominium developments flourished in those same neighborhoods. At the same time, the longstanding racial segregation and inequality in the city's public schools and the loss of thousands of blue-collar jobs for poor and working-class young people of color was a devastating double blow to the economic opportunity outlook for our communities.

At Coleman, we began to wonder aloud about the relevance of a small child advocacy organization in this context. Was there even a future for children in the city? Without vibrant racially and economically diverse neighborhoods with children, extended families, and social networks, what was the future of the city at all? A city for the rich, with its poor and working classes pushed to the outer rings of the region? A city of, by, and for tourists? A city without a soul?

After thirty years, were we powerful enough to turn the tide? What could we do, with a staff of ten, thirty paid youth and parent advocates, a political base of hundreds of child-serving agencies, and a budget of less than $800,000 a year? With determination and hope in our eyes, we said we could have a major impact, but we would have to become an even more powerful voice for families—enough to stand up to well-financed developers and a seemingly intractable school system. And clearly we could not do it alone. We would have to be part of strong strategic alliances; we would have to have long-term vision, long-term plans, and stamina. We would need to mobilize thousands of people around a common agenda and move tens of thousands of voters to the polls on our issues. We would have to be part of building a movement.

As a next-generation leader, I know well the history of social movements despite having never seen one in person. I know that strong grassroots organizations of disenfranchised people are the foundation of all movements and that they require years and decades of dogged day-to-day organizing before the work catches fire and has the capacity to truly make history. I knew that after thirty years of advocacy and organizing for low-income families, Coleman Advocates was on the brink of creating an even more powerful community-driven organization that could help form the foundation of the kind of movement we so urgently need.

To take that next step and seize the opportunity to become the kind of social change organization our families and communities needed, I knew that Coleman would have to grow into its next stage of development.

Child advocacy, race, accountability, and power

At the same time that I was coming into leadership and developing a new analysis of Coleman's role in the changing context of San Francisco, a longstanding issue that faces all advocacy agencies came to the forefront. In the report *Building Bridges: Linking Child Advocacy and Community Organizing Strategies*, David Richart called it "the crisis of representation" facing child advocacy organizations: Who had given Coleman the "permission" to represent the needs of low-income children in the halls of power, most of whom are children of color?[3] How did we know if we were representing low-income families or communities of color fairly? How did we know if our policy agendas reflected their needs and most urgent priorities? When we won victories at city hall, who felt ownership of those victories? And who exactly gained power, access, and visibility that could be leveraged for the next big fight? Whose leadership were we building, and for what purpose? These are fundamental questions about the role of child advocacy organizations in a democracy and about their role in changing, or maintaining, systems of profound racial and economic inequality.

If a core democratic principle is that people directly affected by a problem should have a voice in deciding what to do about it, why are child advocacy organizations staffed by professional, expert advocates with few ties to low-income children and families? Why are board and staff members so often unreflective of the communities they seek to support? Why are there often only token opportunities for low-income parents and young people of color to speak directly to policymakers about their needs? Why do advocates set policy agendas without any significant participation of parents or young people, who know their own needs best?

Thirty years into the development of the child advocacy field, the reality is that many of our organizations have become effective powerhouses capable of winning legislative battles that improve the lives of millions of children, but they will never live up to their democratic promise or help create the kind of systemic social change that poor children and their families need in the long term. We will increase funding for agencies to serve the poor but fail to end poverty. Our vision must be bigger, broader and bolder.

The next generation

When our veteran executive director of twenty-six years, Margaret Brodkin, left Coleman, we took this moment of significant leadership transition as an opportunity to reflect deeply on our work. The end result of more than a year of reflection and strategic planning was a five-year strategic plan that outlined some dramatic new shifts in strategy and focus for the organization. Together the board, staff, youth, and parent leaders of the organization collectively decided to deepen our commitment to youth and parent leadership by moving closer to a traditional community organizing model while maintaining the best of our advocacy roots. We crafted a unique hybrid model, rooted in the theory and practice of community organizing, that pushes our constituency-led empowerment work to the next level, still guided by our own legacy and distinctive brand of pragmatism.

In this fourth, most recent strategy shift, we are creating a remarkably vibrant, democratic, effective, community-driven organizational base of power for the working families of San Francisco. The Coleman of today has a staff that is 100 percent people of color (half of whom are from our constituency) and a base of several hundred family members, 90 percent of whom are very low-income to moderate-income youth and parents of color and overwhelmingly African American and immigrant Latino families. Our building, based in the southeast sector of the city where most working families can afford to live, buzzes with the activity of parent and youth membership meetings, campaign activities, and the voices of scores of children. These families are driving the issues we take on and the tactics we choose, and they are making new kinds of victories possible. In 2006 and 2007, we won more than $20 million in funding for affordable family housing, got the mayor and the board of supervisors to double the city's plans for affordable housing for low-income families in the next four years, won a youth jobs campaign and an "Our Schools, Our Superintendent" campaign to add community input to the superintendent selection process, and put together a $10 million grassroots budget campaign that funded the most urgent priorities of 2000 families surveyed for our multiethnic Budget 4 Families Campaign.

To move in this direction required an intense and highly inclusive planning process that lasted more than a year. We recruited new board members, revised our mission, clarified our constituency and therefore who we were accountable to, explicitly named our long-term vision for the city of San Francisco, and articulated a new set of principles to guide our work. Among the principles were the following:

NEW DIRECTIONS FOR YOUTH DEVELOPMENT • DOI: 10.1002/yd

a. We believe that all people, including parents and young people, have a democratic right to express their voice and exercise their power in the political and economic decisions that affect their lives.
b. We believe that all children have a right to have their basic needs met, to be educated and prepared for full participation in society, and that it is the responsibility of government to ensure that these rights are fully realized.
c. We believe that economic disparities, persistent poverty and structural racism are the major barriers to meeting the needs of families and children.
d. We believe that Coleman should be reflective of and accountable to our diverse constituency.
e. We believe that we must partner with other community organizations to build a *movement* capable of winning long term, systemic social policy change because we cannot achieve our vision alone.[4]

Organizationally these principles lead to a social change approach closer to community organizing models than traditional advocacy models. Given Coleman's growing commitment over the years to organizing young people and parents, moving in this direction was a stretch for us but not a leap.

We believe that an organization whose advocacy agenda and political strategies are determined by professional experts will win policy victories in the short term but will not increase the community's capacity to win fundamental improvements in their conditions over the long term. This is especially true for poor communities of color, for whom the roots of their crises (in housing, child care, health care, youth violence, or academic achievement) are in deeply embedded structures of racial and economic discrimination, inequality, and oppression that have taken centuries to develop and will take many years and strong movements to undo.

On an imagined continuum between 100 percent staff-led professional advocacy (a 1 on a scale of 1 to 10) and 100 percent grassroots member-led community organizing (a 10 on that scale), we decided to move closer to the organizing end, shifting from a 4 to a 6. An organization located around the 3 or 4 marker on this scale, for example, would be led by professional advocates and might mobilize constituents in significant numbers to speak out on behalf of that agenda. In a model based on a 6 or 7, the constituents themselves have formal decision-making power in the organization and set the policy agenda, so that when it is time for action, they are mobilizing themselves and their own community to assert its needs, agenda, and power. For us, this meant investing more resources in parent and youth organizing to increase our base of leadership from a core of about twenty parent and youth advocates (paid) to a volunteer membership base of at least two hundred families and at least twenty unpaid member-leaders willing and able to lead campaigns on behalf of children and families and to keep building the membership to increase our base of power.

To maximize our limited resources under this new, more labor-intensive model, we had to focus on just two major issues that families themselves all over the city had prioritized—affordable housing and public schools—and step back from leading advocacy efforts in the wide range of issues we had been involved with over the years, including child care, youth development services, juvenile justice, recreation and parks, and city budget advocacy. In a city with the second most expensive housing market in the country that was losing thousands of working families every year to less expensive locales, it was not surprising that housing had become parents' number one concern. (The median-priced home in San Francisco is well above $700,000, and the income needed for a family of three to be self-sufficient is over $60,000.) Increasingly a college education is required to earn a living wage in the city, and families seeking upward mobility were losing hope in the city's public school system's ability to ensure children's entrance into higher education.

Our new five-year strategic plan is guided by the vision that in order to increase significantly the educational and economic opportunities for working-class San Francisco families in this critical period of the city's history, families, and the organizations that fight for them, will need more political power than ever before, especially low-income and working-class families of color, including African American families and Asian, Latino, and Pacific Islander immigrants. Tough fights around housing, development, and public schools—major issues in city politics, with deeply entrenched and conflicting interests—are on the horizon. We have borrowed some of the best of community organizing methods, which place a premium on developing strong community leaders who effectively speak for themselves and organize on behalf of their own communities' interests and on winning campaigns that build community power. Organizationally this leads to membership-based building models and democratic methods of organizational decision making rather than hierarchical, corporate-based models of nonprofit management. Having a base of community members who have joined your organization and have power to lead its political agenda and strategy means the organization has some built-in level of accountability and an institutionalized commitment to long-term community building as well as short-term victory.

But these more democratic models have limits. They can get swamped in democratic processes, can be taken over by dominant or difficult community members, and can lack the expertise or resources they need to develop cutting-edge policy proposals. While the best organizers "start with people where they are," organizations too often leave people there, without challenging community members' long-held biases and assumptions. This can lead to a reactionary populism that advocates policies that are actually not in the community's long-term interest. An additional concern for us when moving to an organizing model was that community organizing groups often lack the flexibility to seize moments of political opportunity quickly. Our ability to navigate swiftly through local political waters and respond quickly to a new political landscape has resulted in a number of victories and gives us the credibility to play the inside game.

Because of some of these challenges, in our restructuring we have also maintained some of the most effective elements of the more professional advocacy model. First, to maintain our ability to apply effective inside pressure, we have to institutionalize ways to keep a close eye on city government and communicate to city policymakers that we are watching. We have therefore chosen to continue to write and disseminate our weekly *Advocate Alert* to over three thousand supporters, media, and city officials. In addition, while most of our staff are now organizers in the field, we have maintained an investment in professional staff who have expertise in our core issue areas and are credible opinion leaders in the community and city politics on these issues. We have maintained space for staff to function as advocates and leaders in their issue areas but have put clear boundaries around their individual authority. Finally, to balance grassroots leadership with effective policy analysis and strategy, we have implemented an organizational agenda-setting process that is research driven, member led, and guided strongly by staff but must be approved by the entire membership and the board of directors. Between 2006 and 2007, our Affordable Family Housing Platform and Education Equity Platforms were developed by our youth and parent organizing committees, with strong staff research support, but approved at meetings of the entire organization (one had about fifty people, the other more than a hundred). The parent and youth organizing committees then choose campaigns within these broad platforms.

Despite the difficult times facing our communities, our country, and indeed the planet, I believe that a more humane, peaceful, and just society for all our children is possible. I believe, like many others of my generation, that the leaders who will have the courage, creativity, and tenacity to create the change we so urgently need will not look like the leaders of yesterday or the leaders of many traditional nonprofit advocacy organizations. They are the current, local leaders in our own organizations: immigrant parents from Mexico, young black people raised in public housing, struggling white single mothers. Their own future is at stake, and they are ready for the struggle.

Notes

1. For a discussion of these issues, see Marsh, D. S., & Daniel, M. H. (2003). *Leadership for policy change*. Oakland, CA: Policy Link.

2. See www.dcyf.org for more information about the department's current work.

3. Richart, D. W. (2001). *Building bridges: Linking child advocacy and community organizing strategies to improve children's interests.* Louisville, KY: National Institute on Children, Youth & Families at Spalding University.
4. Coleman Advocates for Children and Youth. *Five year strategic plan: A new framework for our work, 2006–2011.*

NTANYA LEE *has been an activist for social justice since age thirteen and became the executive director of Coleman Advocates for Children and Youth in 2004.*

Parents participating in a community-based organization exhibit the development of increased civic engagement and moral leadership.

5

The development of collective moral leadership among parents through education organizing

Michael P. Evans, Dennis Shirley

JUST OFF THE FREEDOM TRAIL in Boston and directly behind the Old State House is 26 Court Street, home to the central offices of the Boston Public Schools (BPS). Inside, the Edward Winters Chamber plays host to the bimonthly BPS School Committee (BSC) meetings. The seven-member committee sits, facing the public, behind a large curved bench with Interim Superintendent Michael Contompasis and chair Elizabeth Reilinger occupying the two middle seats. Positioned directly in front of the bench is a small table with two chairs and a microphone that members of the public use to address the committee. Only one or two individuals generally occupy the table, but during the BPS budget meeting on March 21, 2007, twelve concerned citizens gathered to make a statement to the BSC. These individuals represented a number of community-based organizations (CBOs) in Boston that were advocating for the reallocation of funds to hire additional family and community outreach coordinators (FCOCs) in schools across the

NEW DIRECTIONS FOR YOUTH DEVELOPMENT, NO. 117, SPRING 2008 © WILEY PERIODICALS, INC.
Published online in Wiley InterScience (www.interscience.wiley.com) • DOI: 10.1002/yd.248

district. Holding signs with group names and slogans such as "Sociedad Latina Supports FCOCs" and "JP-POP for FCOCs," they crowded behind Caprice Taylor Mendez, director of the Boston Parent Organizing Network (BPON). "I am humbled to have been selected to represent the families who worked so hard to bring additional FCOCs into the Boston schools," she began. "Low income families and parents for whom English is not their first language are traditionally labeled as disengaged, and by raising their voices to ask for more FCOCs they are showing their commitment to improve their children's lives."[1] This dramatic presentation marked the culmination of a spring campaign that included months of prior planning, the creation and circulation of a campaign issue newsletter, BPON news blasts over e-mail listservs, parents' testimonies at public hearings, and telephone calls and letters to Boston School Committee members, Boston mayor Thomas Menino, and city councilors.[2]

As a result of the advocacy of these CBOs, the BSC unanimously approved Contampasis's revised budget for fiscal year 2008, including the reallocation of $385,000 for hiring six additional FCOCs and one additional staff member for the Office of Community and Family Engagement. This almost doubled the number of family and community engagement personnel from seventeen to thirty-two and brought the funding total to $825,000. During the meeting, Interim Superintendent Contampasis commented on the decision to increase funding: "We have had the benefit of three public hearings on the budget. I am grateful to those parents, teachers and other members of the community who took the time to attend the hearings and provide testimony. The one consistent theme that we heard throughout these hearings was the effectiveness of and the need for additional Family and Community Outreach Coordinators."[3] Although this was certainly an important victory, BPON and its affiliates will continue to work toward their eventual goal of having an FCOC in every school in the city school system.

Notably many of the individuals who gave testimony in the 2007 hearings already had FCOCs working in their children's schools. However, as members of CBOs, they felt compelled to share their experiences and work for the betterment of the educational system as a whole. As we spoke with these parents after the hearings, it was clear that while they recognized the interconnectivity between the success of the entire system and their child's education, they also felt that their participation was a moral imperative. They had learned to act beyond their individual self-interest to organize on behalf of the entire community. These attitudes and actions are vastly different from the common depiction of parental involvement, where individual parents are described as working primarily for the benefit of their own child.

This transition from acting as an individual self-interested client to a community leader with an explicit ethical commitment is, we suggest, more latent than overt in much of the scholarship on community organizing. In fact, some organizing groups seem to consider the ethical dimensions of individuals to be inherently suspect.[4] Yet our research findings point in another direction—one that suggests that parents understand their moral growth to be an important part of their development as community advocates.

To advance this claim, we turn to the experiences of members of the Jamaica Plain Parent Organizing Project (JP-POP). We present qualitative data from interviews with JP-POP members to ascertain the motivations behind their initial decisions to become involved in education, the benefits they derive from their participation, and the gradual evolution of narrow definitions of self-interest to more communal understandings. Finally, we draw out implications for the potential capacity enhancement of CBOs in education at both the institutional and district levels.

Traditional depictions of parent participation

Family involvement is traditionally understood as a schoolcentric endeavor—one in which the duty of the family is to serve the interests of the broader school community. Hence many reforms are focused on changing the behaviors of parents and families.[5] This is in stark contrast to the blunt emphasis on power and self-interest traditionally promoted by many CBOs. For example, Saul Alinsky, generally considered the father of community organizing, contended that in spite of lofty rhetoric about idealism, everyone ultimately operates out of self-interest. He refused to allow people, especially those in power, to ground their motives in moral jargon. As far as he was concerned, such talk was simply window dressing for self-interest: "We repeatedly get caught in this conflict between our professed moral principles and the real reason why we do things—to wit, our self-interest. We are always able to mask those real reasons in words of beneficent goodness—freedom justice, and so on."[6]

Today hundreds of CBOs across the United States continue to study and draw on core principles of Alinsky organizing, and group training sessions often emphasize power analyses and studies of power holders' interests. Yet what actually happens when organizations fail to appeal to individuals' higher aspirations for moral purpose and community solidarity? If individuals are involved only out of self-interest, what will keep them involved when their individual needs are met? Furthermore, how can groups avoid becoming insular and continue to conduct outreach to the community?

In response to these questions, contemporary organizing has evolved to recognize the importance of relational organizing, that is, bringing people with shared values together to discuss community needs. This has been particularly effective in congregationally based community organizing, as practiced by the Industrial Areas Foundation and the Pacific Institute for Community Organizing (PICO).[7] Yet it may also be the case that the human quest for moral purpose and community solidarity hardly is limited to those who come to organizing out of different faith traditions. How might a sense of moral purpose be generated in community organizations that lack an explicit faith-based orientation? What might the relationship be between an initial preoccupation with the self or one's family and a broader commitment to community welfare and social justice? With these questions in mind, we consider in greater detail the growth of parents' community advocacy for youth in the instance of JP-POP.

Jamaica Plain—Parent Organizing Project

Officially JP-POP is a program housed within a larger community organization known as City Life/Vida Urbana (CLVU). In 2002, JP-POP was formed as a subsidiary of CLVU with a primary focus on education and especially on the needs of bilingual learners and children with special needs. JP-POP is also one of thirty-six member organizations that make up the Boston Parent Organizing Network (BPON). Established in 1999, BPON's primary role is to help facilitate the sharing of information, ideas, and strategies among member organizations. In addition, it provides some grant funding, and JP-POP is one of the major recipients.

Although membership in JP-POP is open to anyone, participants are primarily low-income, Spanish-speaking women representing the Boston neighborhoods of Jamaica Plain, Roslindale, Hyde Park, South Boston, Roxbury, and Dorchester. Most members have children with moderate to severe special needs. The group has developed an expertise in this area, and many parents first become aware of JP-POP through word of mouth from other parents or teachers. It is also worth noting that because of Boston's current student assignment plan, the children of the JP-POP members do not necessarily attend neighborhood schools. In fact, most travel to other neighborhoods in the city. Therefore, parents living in separate parts of the city may have children in the same school, while the children of next-door neighbors may be spread across the city. This has traditionally been an obstacle to education organizing efforts in Boston and contributes to the geographical diversity of JP-POP's membership.

Becoming involved in JP-POP

Members reported in interviews that prior to their involvement in JP-POP, their participation in schools varied from heavily involved room parents to those who rarely visited their child's campus. Involved parents cited invitations to school events, school communications in their native language, and the outreach efforts of individual teachers and administrators as key components in the creation of a welcoming school culture. One involved parent stated, "My son's first-grade teacher was excellent. She was always sending notes home saying, 'This week we worked on this, this, and this. I want you to help by practicing some of these things at home.' This was excellent." However, maintaining close connections with school was often a challenge, even for those who were deeply committed to staying involved. The common sentiment was that schools would keep parents informed only about activities that support their own agenda and that additional efforts must be made to become aware of all of the issues at a school. For example, one parent described her disappointment when she learned from the bus monitor that there would be one fewer classroom aide the following year, a necessary requirement according to her son's individual educational plan (IEP):

The schools don't always inform the parents of their rights. And I am very involved, you can go and ask the principal and she will say, "Oh, they are always here, they are good parents." But the school still didn't tell me about the bus issue; I had to find out from the old lady who was riding with my son. I couldn't believe it! If this can happen to me, I have to wonder about the parents who have to go to work or who can't be at the school all the time.

Other participants described limited prior involvement with schools. Unfortunately a disconnect between home and school is common among immigrant, minority, and working-class families, who frequently feel like outsiders to the educational process.[8] Research indicates that these families are often hindered by some combination of linguistic, economic, or cultural barriers that engender misunderstandings among teachers and school personnel. Among JP-POP participants, the most commonly cited obstacles to involvement were language and cultural differences.

The linguistic issue went beyond the inability to effectively communicate. In interviews parents expressed a range of emotions including fear, anger, and sadness. For example, one parent said, "I felt scared going to school. Like I didn't belong. It was a very foreign place." And another commented, "I feel sad and stupid; it seems like they don't take into consideration the needs of the Hispanic families in the community. They don't consider our right. Sometimes I feel that there is an attitude that Hispanic parents don't want to get involved, but this isn't so. Even when there is a translator, it is hard, because you can't really pay attention. You have to listen to the translation, and you can't focus on the speaker."

Another major barrier concerned cultural differences in the relationships between home and school. The majority of JP-POP parents did not attend school in the United States and lacked experience with the traditional social relationships that exist in American education. All of the parents described school relationships in their own country as being grounded in trust. Although they were quick to acknowledge many of the educational shortcomings of their native educational systems, it was also assumed that the school staff at home always had the best interest of the children in mind. One mother from the Dominican Republic described the relationships at home in familial terms: "At home the teacher is like a second mother. We were taught that they were always right. So when I came to the United States, I always assumed that the teacher was always right, but I have learned that I need to listen to my child as well." Initial high levels of trust kept parents away from schools, but ironically, what was intended as an act of respect on the behalf of parents could be interpreted as a lack of commitment by American teachers.

All of the parents who were interviewed, regardless of their level of involvement, expressed a desire to support both their child and the school staff. Frequently it was the realization that their child's needs were not being met that motivated them to initiate contact with a CBO like JP-POP. Parents could often point to a particularly frustrating or challenging incident that forced them to seek additional help. Often it was the difficulties that they faced in acquiring services for a child with special needs. One mother with an autistic son said, "It is really difficult being a parent of a child with special needs. You really have to educate yourself and learn how to advocate for them so that they can at least get the minimum of the services. It can be very frustrating." There was also a concern that their child might slip through the cracks if they did not become more adept at navigating the educational system, and several of the parents were motivated by their inability to assist their older children and were determined that their younger children would get the education that they deserve. As one mother remarked:

Without resources it is very difficult to support your child. Before I knew how to advocate for myself, my daughter went through the entire school system and graduated without learning how to read. Now I am working to make sure that the same thing does not happen with my son. Now I know how to advocate for myself. Now I feel that I can go wherever I need to go to deal with my child's situation.

Although self-interest and the desire to meet the immediate needs of their children are the primary motivating factors for joining JP-POP, members quickly come to appreciate through their participation multiple benefits of working with a CBO.

Participation in JP-POP: Building knowledge, support, and confidence

Participants rarely knew what to expect when they began their participation with JP-POP, and several expressed some initial hesitation. Many of the parents had previously been disappointed with other organizations that inundated them with information and left them feeling lost and confused. In JP-POP they quickly learned that their personal experiences would be central to the group's activities. In describing the benefits that were derived through their participation, three interrelated themes emerged that we categorize as the development of knowledge, the creation of a network of support, and the engenderment of feelings of empowerment through increased confidence. We consider these three themes in their interdependence with one another to be central to the creation of collective moral leadership of parents in JP-POP.

Knowledge

Building and creating knowledge to empower members is a central part of JP-POP's mission. The learning that takes place is accomplished through the sharing of technical, social, and practical expertise. Here we are defining *technical knowledge* as the specialized information that is commonly the domain of professionals, *social knowledge* as the information collectively gathered by the community, and *practical knowledge* as the application of knowledge in action. Of course, in practice, these three elements are not discrete, but instead supplement one another, enhancing the overall utility of the acquired information as a tool for achieving objectives.

The technical knowledge often included step-by-step instructions from legal and educational experts.[9] These opportunities were occasionally provided by JP-POP, but members frequently attended events and workshops sponsored by BPS or other advocacy groups. Whenever possible, JP-POP tried to make sure that translation would be available and the information was provided in Spanish. In addition to relying on legal or educational experts, the parents themselves often became valuable resources for the group. Many of the parents are involved with other organizations that specifically address their child's needs. This contributes to the sum communal knowledge of the group. As one member remarked, "It is great because we each go to other workshops and collect resources that we bring back and share with the group." For example, at one monthly meeting, a mother was observed patiently providing a detailed explanation of Asperger's syndrome to a relatively new member of JP-POP. Her description included the place of Asperger's on the autism spectrum, common symptoms, and some specific strategies that could be implemented in the classroom. This individual's child had been diagnosed with Pervasive Development Disorder–Not Otherwise Specified (PDD-NOS), but she had learned about Asperger's during the diagnostic process and while attending various workshops on autism. Now she was able to share her knowledge clearly and concisely.

Social connections are also crucial to the success of the group. This is especially true in Boston, where more traditional neighborhood networks may be thwarted by the school assignment policy. Through the connections of the JP-POP members, they are able to achieve a broader awareness of Boston's education landscape. One member commented, "People get to know about a school, and they share their knowledge. It works out because there is someone you can turn to if you need to get information or if you are looking for someone to talk to." If there are opportunities made available in the district, such as conferences, parent-training sessions, or public meetings, at least one of the members will likely hear about it and share with the rest of the group.

Finally, organization members learn how to apply the knowledge that they have acquired. This is particularly helpful in a vast bureaucratic system like BPS. For example, in one workshop, the guest speaker was listing the names of some individuals to contact at BPS. As one name appeared on the dry erase board, a JP-POP member said, "Oh, she never answers her phone. She is almost impossible to get a hold of." Another parent sitting across the room said, "Yes, but you can call Carol [a pseudonym] who is in the office next door. Ask her to poke her head into the office and tell her to pick up the phone before you call." This type of insider information is acquired through experience and swapped freely among the parents. One mother remarked, "You learn as you live it. Then you can share this information with the others in the group, and they share what they have experienced." Together the JP-POP parents feel that they have enough information to navigate the school system successfully.

Support

In addition to the knowledge that is acquired, JP-POP also serves as a support network. The parents have often shared frustrating and challenging situations and are able to lean on one another during difficult times. This personal element might not be achieved through traditional professional organizations, and it makes a big difference. One member said, "Having other parents there talking about similar issues that they are facing, to be honest with you, I feel renewed by the end of the meeting." Another stated, "We learn from each other. Not only is the learning important, but we are also able to serve as a support group. Sometimes I think that I am going through a tough situation, but then I hear that someone else is going through an even worse situation. It really helps that we are able to listen to one another."

Perhaps the most powerful demonstration of mutual support is the common practice of attending IEP meetings with one another. The participants are there to offer support and to serve as another set of eyes and ears. These meetings can be stressful, and several participants described feeling overwhelmed by the amount of information exchanged in these conversations. The assessment of a child's learning disabilities usually entails the use of instruments requiring educators' professional expertise, and parents can easily become uncertain as to the significance of rating scales of statistical results.

It is at this juncture that the socialized knowledge of other JP-POP parents is crucial. Parents report that when they attend IEP meetings at schools with other members, "We listen and support one another. On occasion we might remind someone of an important question to ask, and afterward we always sit down and talk about the meeting. We compare notes, develop follow-up questions, and decide on the next course of action." While some educators might be surprised and intimidated by a group of parents attending an IEP meeting, which traditionally includes only the primary guardian, the presence of the additional JP-POP members is simply intended to provide "support for one another through the process." One member described a situation in which "there was even more JP-POP parents at a meeting than school officials." Even for parents who are well informed about the IEP process, the presence of other parents is much appreciated. As one new member remarked, "These meetings have always been very emotional for me because we are talking about my child, so it really helps to have someone else there to support me."

The support that parents provide for one another at IEP meetings provides an intriguing example of what Lave and Wenger describe as "legitimate peripheral participation."[10] Parents with similar questions about the BPS and the classification of their children as learning disabled provide emotional support for one another, learn how to share information and conduct advocacy for their children, and network with other CBOs across the district. The relationships between parents are primarily public in nature rather than informal friendships. On parent commented, "Maybe we don't socialize together, but still we are very tight as a group. As a group we can pick an issue and agree that this is what we are going to do. As a group we are very strong."

Confidence

Finally, because of the knowledge that they have gained and the support that they receive from one another, participants experienced an increased sense of confidence that enabled them to become more active participants in their children's schooling. They began by attending meetings and workshops and learning by observing others participate or giving testimony. As they grew more secure in this role, they began to participate more in meetings, and many eventually moved on to present their own testimonies. New members practice with more experienced members so that they feel better prepared when talking to teachers, principals, the school committee, or even the mayor. One parent described the pinnacle of her transformation from timid parent to confident advocate as follows:

I used to be afraid to go to the school and I wouldn't talk to anyone at the school. But now that I know what my rights are, I realize that I need to speak up to advocate for my son. Before I was afraid, but not anymore. A few weeks ago I was at a meeting with my son's teacher, and he called him a liar. I felt really insulted, and after the meeting I sent my son out of the room and told the teacher how I felt. I said that his language was setting a poor example for my son, who is trying to become less aggressive. The teacher acknowledged this, and he actually apologized. I never would have done something like that prior to joining JP-POP, I would have been too afraid. I really feel empowered to speak up.

With new-found knowledge, support, and confidence, members feel better prepared to meet the needs of their children. And as a result of their participation, they also come to recognize how their individual concerns are linked to the needs of the broader community, and their narrow self-interests become more broadly defined.

Conclusion: The emergence of collective moral leadership

While the immediate needs of their children was a common starting place for the involvement of parents, their immersion in the JP-POP community keeps parents coming back and has broadened their perception of what it means to conduct advocacy work for children. Virtually every parent entered the relationship with JP-POP because of concerns with an individual child. Yet while meeting the needs of their own children was cited as important, they now understand that "what is good for the community is good for my child." Parents increasingly understand that engaging in campaigns that do not have a direct impact on their children is part of their collective moral leadership, as was demonstrated by the participation of parents who already have FCOCs in the 2007 campaign.

In part, this commitment stems from a new sense of moral responsibility and community accountability to one another. Many members demonstrated strong devotion to JP-POP; its growth and success have become a priority in their lives. One member stated, "Now I try to get involved with everything at City Life. I attend everything, and now I am learning about other issues like housing. Even if they call me at the last minute, I wouldn't say no. I wouldn't dare say no, because of how they have helped me with my son. I have left other appointments just to support City Life events." Even when there are internal disagreements, members can be counted on to support one another. Several members indicated that they planned to remain involved in JP-POP even after their children completed school.

As school districts continue their struggle to improve educational opportunities for all children, CBOs like JP-POP should be looked to as potentially powerful allies for enacting sustainable change. In an era when federal legislation like No Child Left Behind is offering families more exit strategies from public education, community group members may serve as a solid foundation of support that both challenge urban districts and make them efficacious by moving from islands of bureaucracy to centers of civic engagement.[11] Research indicates that in terms of working with marginalized populations, experienced teachers may have greater knowledge of the obstacles that parents face, but they remain unaware of potential community resources.[12] Teachers who are able to tap into community funds of knowledge report better communication with parents and deeper connections with their students.[13]

These research findings suggest that scholars should look more closely at the relationship of educators, parents, and CBOs. Community organizers who are working in the area of school improvement might wish to reconsider their historical emphasis on self-interest, or at least relate it to a broader sense of moral purpose that is likely to appeal to educators and is compatible with their sense of vocational calling. Educators should understand that CBOs can help individual parents to evolve beyond a sense of clients with individual agendas to advocates with well-honed political skills who are concerned with the well-being of all of the children in their community. As the history of the civil rights movement in particular shows, idealism and moral purpose constitute powerful psychic resources that can generate group membership, galvanize community solidarity, and catalyze powerful social movements that overturn decades of the most grievous social inequalities.[14] If education organizing is to continue to develop, deliberate, targeted reflection about ways to capitalize on this psychic resource at this moment in history is warranted.

Notes

1. The quotations are based on observations from the March 21, 2007, Boston School Committee meeting and the March 22, 2007, BPON press

release, *BPS doubles number of schools with families as partners to close the achievement gap.*

2. For a sample of the campaign materials see *Parent leaders in action,* 7(1), www.bpon.org.

3. Evan, M. P. Field notes, March 21, 2007.

4. Shirley, D. (1997). *Community organizing for urban school reform.* Austin: University of Texas Press; Shirley, D. (2002). *Valley interfaith and school reform: Organizing for power in south Texas.* Austin: University of Texas Press.

5. Schutz, A. (2006). Home is a prison in the global city: The tragic failure of school-based community engagement strategies. *Review of Educational Research,* 76(4), 691–743.

6. Alinsky, S. D. (1971). *Rules for radicals: A pragmatic primer for realistic radicals.* New York: Vintage. P. 58.

7. For an examination of Industrial Areas Foundation work, see Shirley, D. (1997, 2002); Warren, M. R. (2001). *Dry bones rattling: Community building to revitalize American democracy.* Princeton, NJ: Princeton University Press. For PICO, see Wood, R. L. (2002). *Faith in action: Religion, race, and democratic organizing in America.* Chicago: University of Chicago Press.

8. Lareau, A., & Horvat, E. M. (1999). Moments of social inclusion and exclusion: Race, class and cultural capital in family-school relationships. *Sociology of Education,* 72(1), 37–53.

9. For example, two observations included presentations by a member of the Ed Law Project: http://www.youthadvocacyproject.org/edlaw/edlaw.htm.

10. Lave, J., & Wenger, E. (1991). *Situated learning: Legitimate peripheral participation.* Cambridge: Cambridge University Press.

11. Oakes, J., & Rogers, J. (2006). *Learning power: Organizing for education and justice.* New York: Teachers College Press; Rogers, J. (2006). Forces of accountability: The power of parents in NCLB. *Harvard Educational Review,* 76(4), 611–641.

12. Shunow, L., & Harris, W. (2000). Teachers thinking about home-school relations in low-income urban communities. *School Community Journal,* 10(1), 9–24.

13. Moll, L. C., Amanti, C., Neff, D., & Gonzales, N. (1992). Funds of knowledge for teaching: Using a qualitative approach to connect homes and classrooms. *Theory into Practice,* 31(2), 132–140; Moll, L. C., & Greenberg, J. B. (1990). Creating zones of possibilities: Combining social contexts for instruction. In L. C. Moll (Ed.), *Vygotsky and education: Instructional implications and applications of sociohistorical psychology.* Cambridge: Cambridge University Press.

14. Payne, C. M. (1997). *I've got the light of freedom: The organizing tradition and the Mississippi freedom struggle.* Berkeley: University of California Press.

MICHAEL P. EVANS *is a doctoral candidate in curriculum and instruction at the Lynch School of Education at Boston College.*

DENNIS SHIRLEY *is professor of education at the Lynch School of Education at Boston College.*

Oakland Community Organizations has engaged in parent organizing for education reform for over ten years. This article details OCO's strategies, challenges, and accomplishments.

6

Faith-based organizing for youth: One organization's district campaign for small schools policy

Ron Snyder

IN 1996 OAKLAND COMMUNITY ORGANIZATIONS (OCO) initiated an education reform campaign to transform the Oakland Unified School District in Oakland, California, so that every family would have a choice for a quality school.[1] We envisioned that children would be known by their names and would have the support of an adult community to develop to their fullest potential, preparing them for college, career, and citizenship. Since then, OCO leaders have created a grassroots movement responsible for the creation of forty new small schools and ten small charters across Oakland, new school facilities in which to house them, stronger parent engagement, and better outcomes for children. This article describes OCO's organizing and advocacy work to achieve these results and examines the role of parent self-interest, political positioning, and the leverage, alliances, and action that led to successful advocacy.

Leaders of OCO began their work on education reform through hundreds of one-to-one conversations to learn the concerns of

WILEY InterScience® DISCOVER SOMETHING GREAT
NEW DIRECTIONS FOR YOUTH DEVELOPMENT, NO. 117, SPRING 2008 © WILEY PERIODICALS, INC.
Published online in Wiley InterScience (www.interscience.wiley.com) • DOI: 10.1002/yd.249

parents, teachers, and community residents. They heard frustration and anger about unsafe, dirty, overcrowded, and underperforming schools. Despite Oakland's population growth, the school district had failed to build a new school in thirty years. Schools originally built for six hundred to seven hundred students were serving a thousand to as many as fourteen hundred. Oakland schools ranked among the lowest in the state, and many students were dropping out. Children of color and children living in low-income communities carried the brunt of this grave injustice. Parents and community leaders knew they needed something better for their children.

To date, thousands of parents, along with hundreds of teachers, have undertaken the hard work necessary to improve educational opportunities for Oakland's lowest-achieving students. Oakland Community Organizations is making a place for parents in the education of their children and rekindling hope in teachers and administrators. Over the past year, its leaders have worked in thirty-one small schools and charter schools to bring about meaningful and sustainable parent engagement and improved student outcomes through the small schools movement.

Understanding parent organizing in an urban context

Ordinary people understand the source of parental advocacy to be love. From the beginning to the end, most parents act out of their deep love for their child. For OCO, the key to effective organizing and advocacy for youth is to agitate the individual and collective response to the question, "Whom do you love?" We call this self-interest. As we OCO leaders sort through our own motivations and those of others and make judgments about tactics to achieve our ends, we have left ourselves open to be judged by our faithfulness to our values through this same question: "Whom do you love?"

Although we have involved large numbers of young people in education reform, OCO primarily develops adult leaders. Therefore, education organizing is from the perspective of adult advocacy on behalf of children. There are many forms of educational

advocacy: political organizing, volunteer work, school site governance, student advocacy, and academic support. In our observation,
parents with advantage or privilege (those who are white or afflu-
ent, or both) naturally feel entitled to operate at every level. Most
parents with less formal education, those without English as their
primary language, or immigrants or poor parents of color do not
easily move into any of these arenas of advocacy. Stories about successful advocacy in low-income communities of color tend to focus
on the individual hero: the principal who transforms the inner-city
school, a teacher who gets all of his or her students to pass the
Advance Placement class, or the exceptional student who over-
comes immense odds to become successful. Oakland Community
Organizations goes beyond examples of individual success by developing leaders from communities that do not have easy access to
power and supporting them while they learn the skills and gain the
confidence to act successfully on behalf of their children, individ-
ually and collectively.

Oakland Community Organizations increases parents' ability
to advocate at every level, focusing primarily on the political
arena. Using the Pacific Institute for Community Organizing
(PICO) National Network method, we empower individuals
through a collective faith-based model of organizing that
emphasizes shared principles and a process for leadership development and is grounded in local institutions. As people grow in
their understanding and ability to lead in the public arena, they
also apply their learning in personal, interpersonal, systemic,
and institutional settings. The PICO model is built on the principle that power is a product of relationships and that building
relationships of trust through face-to-face visits and house
meetings allows people to move together. With staff support,
leaders use research to document issues and develop solutions
for commonly held concerns. Research is followed by large
action meetings where commitments to solutions are negotiated
with public officials and witnessed by the community, demonstrating power that continues to expand as the process repeats
itself over time.

Organizing context

Oakland Community Organizations develops effective leaders within the context of the city of Oakland, taking into consideration the city's demographics and political environment. Of Oakland's nearly 400,000 residents, almost 20 percent are foreign born, 15.5 percent are Asian, 21.89 percent are Hispanic/Latino of any race, 36 percent are African American, 31 percent are white, and 12 percent are other, leaving no racial or ethnic majority. Only 35 percent of Oakland's residents are home owners, and the poverty rate is nearly 20 percent. Thirty-one thousand of the school district's 46,000 students qualified for free or reduced-cost lunch in 2006.

OCO leaders are from congregations and schools located in Oakland's low-income neighborhoods. Oakland's politics are liberal to left by most definitions. The need for education reform is well documented in Oakland and across the rest of California. As OCO leaders push the Oakland education reform effort, we know that economic and social conditions need to be considered if our work is to have lasting impact. We continually refine our organizing strategy to address both immediate and long-term needs by the many Oakland families and students who have poor educational options.

Organizing for better education in Oakland

After successful OCO campaigns resulting in programmatic improvements including class-size reduction, after-school programs, and school-to-career academies, OCO staff and leaders were not satisfied with results, so they continued to search for systemic approaches consistent with our organizing model that would get sustainable educational improvement for our children and their families.

Phase I: Planting the seeds for a movement

Oakland Community Organizations' small schools movement began in 1999 with conversations in people's homes (our model describes these as "one-to-ones") where OCO organizers asked parents about their children's experiences in school. These conversations quickly moved to groups of mothers and a few fathers gathering in the church hall while their children were in Bible school. Led by parents with the support of an organizer, the conversations, in the words of OCO leader Lillian Lopez, became deeply meaningful: "This is the first honest discussion we had in all my years of being in the PTA or School Site Council. We finally talked about more than dirty bathrooms and playground fights or rubberstamping the principal's budget. We talked about whether our kids can read. I was scared to death that my last son was going to drop out of school like his older brother."

The first transformation in parents' sense of empowerment is internal, but the journey to change conditions cannot be taken alone. The one-to-one conversations and formal training help leaders learn how to develop their understanding, skill, and emotional intelligence to become organizational leaders and individual advocates. After every experience or activity, it is the job of the organizer or a veteran leader to reflect on that experience and draw out self-understanding, social dynamics, and challenges for the next step in the journey.

Tapping into the stories of pain draws people into the discussion. What is necessary to keep and develop leaders is clarity that organizing and leading people will bring about real change. The easiest organizing is about opposing something. Oakland Community Organizations' work is about building something new. Oakland's Jefferson Elementary is a case in point. Reading and research led to the conclusion that overcrowding at the school was a critical cause of many of the problems, from dirty bathrooms to school yard fights and, most important, student failure. Built for eight hundred students, the school now housed twelve hundred. The school ran on a year-round schedule requiring students and teachers to use several days each quarter to pack up and move to a new classroom resulting in the loss of more than thirty days of instruction time. Because one-fourth of the teachers were always on vacation, staff did not know each other and it was impossible to build a cohesive team. Equipped with this evidence and supported by data, parents reached out to teachers and the principal and asked to create a small school pilot on one corner of the campus. Opposition from the teachers' union and the district defeated this first request. We had love but no leverage. Effective advocacy requires strategic use of political leverage.

Leaders at OCO decided to build momentum through deeper research. To understand more fully the power of the ideas behind small schools, twenty OCO leaders traveled to New York City to District 2 in Harlem to see small schools in action. They concluded that change could not take place one school at a time because pilot projects could be washed away at any moment. We needed to change district policy. When the petition to pilot a small school at Jefferson was turned down a second time, OCO pursued the idea of opening charter schools as a preliminary strategy in developing small, autonomous, parent-engaged schools. Parents quickly organized parent meetings in congregations across East Oakland, tapping into feelings about how their children were doing and sharing information about size and test scores. Two critical factors helped build the leverage needed to get the attention of the school district: the role of faith institutions and a landmark piece of research comparing hills schools (those of the wealthier families in the city) and flatland schools (where most of the low-income children went) regarding size and test scores.

After researching the pros and cons of charter schools, six parent groups worked with charter management groups to write charter applications. A critical factor in moving this forward was the interest of churches in playing a vital role in education reform efforts, building on the long history of advocacy for public education in the African American community. The biggest challenge beyond politics was finding adequate facilities. A number of clergy had existing school facilities and were willing to support parents who wanted better public school options. After several months of parent-led small meetings with school board members and public actions involving thousands of parents, the school board approved the six charter proposals developed by OCO leaders. Ultimately three charter schools opened in this first round.

Approval of these charters gave us important leverage to reengage the school district around opening small schools in the district. Oakland's new mayor, Jerry Brown, had just been elected with a huge majority and was a vocal supporter of charter schools. The superintendent of the Oakland Unified School District, Carol Quan, had been fired by the school board, and Brown had his assistant city manager named as interim superintendent. With OCO support, voters had just passed a school facilities bond, part of which would be used to build new schools. The window of opportunity to do something new in Oakland was open. Successful advocacy requires good judgment about political opportunity.

Working with this opportunity, we began a relationship with the Bay Area Coalition for Equitable Schools (BayCES), which added the credential of educational expertise to the community power of OCO. Together we wrote a small schools policy requiring the school district to open ten new small, autonomous schools. We had congregational and parent support but needed teacher allies to overcome anticipated opposition. In the summer of 1999, we reached out to over two hundred teachers in one-to-one conversations to listen to their pain and examine whether their vocational love for children could be recaptured through the idea of small schools. We found support.

That same year, an OCO action at St. Elizabeth Parish involving two thousand parents and leaders gained commitments to a small schools policy and construction of new small school facilities from all major political players in Oakland: Mayor Brown, State Senator Don Perata, City Council President Ignacio de la Fuente, and school board members. That policy was passed in May 2001. Creating new schools was strenuous work, and many parents moved from political advocacy to working with charter companies, interested teachers or principals, and education partners like BayCES to begin the design of the new schools. Countless meetings took place: we designed and found space for new schools and dealt with the logistics of getting the district to follow through on everything from education code numbers to finding desks and textbooks. In fall 2001, five new schools opened.

A critical understanding of organizing is that system change does not easily come from inside the system. Individual advocacy to make existing systems work can be effective from the inside, but system change requires leverage from the outside. Congregations provided a stable institutional base outside the school system from which to leverage change. In addition, congregations provided powerful language and symbols for the moral high ground of equity for children. Powerful ideas presented in powerful ways by leaders representing the power of an organized community won powerful results.

Phase II: Partnership as a form of advocacy: Organizing from the inside

In the landscape of urban school systems, most reform efforts come from the top down by strong superintendents and more recently by mayors who take over school systems. Following the tragic murder of Marcus Foster in 1973, Oakland had several superintendents who each initiated their own programmatic reform. But in 2001, a new superintendent, Dennis Chaconas, was hired who was recognized for both academic and political reasons as an important ally with OCO, which gave us the chance to advocate for systemwide reform. BayCES provided the research and support to help design and support new small schools. The Bill and Melinda Gates Foundation invested $17 million in this effort to develop small schools in the shared belief that they are a critical strategy for improving and reforming education. With the confluence of these forces, OCO leaders began to see their organization as not only a political force that originated this effort but perhaps the guardian angel protecting small school reform.

With OUSD and BayCES and with the support of the Gates Foundation and other funders, OCO was able to build the momentum to create another nine new schools over the next two years. Many OCO parents moved their advocacy from the outside political environment to the inside through parent engagement in roles of governance, volunteerism, and academic support in the emerging small schools. OCO provided leadership training and support in schools where principals requested our assistance. From the perspective of an internal partner, we were able to advocate without public action for powerful ideas that promoted equity.

But internal partnerships do not guarantee that all things go smoothly. A consequence of Gates Foundation funding required

OCO to support the strategy to break large, comprehensive high schools into small schools. These conversions did not build on organized constituents' desire for change. Our interest in supporting system reform meant we could not allow this critical strategy to fail, so we invested staff resources into organizing strategies at the high school level. What we found were incredibly difficult environments. Teachers felt disempowered and resistant to change. Parents felt uninvited and unwelcome. Their students did not want them at school, and neither did school site staff. There were also strong racial divisions at parent and student levels that led to battles for power among adults and conflict and violence between students. OCO organizers played a critical role in response to these conditions.

At Castlemont High, for instance, OCO organizers engaged two local pastors to discuss the possibility of addressing their congregations' issues through the small schools' promise of a safer environment and better student outcomes. An alliance was born, and five hundred African American and Latino leaders secured the commitment from the school district administration and principal to transform Castlemont into small schools. The OCO action created the political will and political cover to undertake this reform over the objections of teachers and others who resisted change. Since then, OCO has been involved at Castlemont, coaching principals, teachers, parents, and students in how to build a relational culture at the school.

In this second phase of advocacy, we moved much of our work to inside the system via partnerships at the school site and district levels. Maintaining the partnership with the school district and others while organizing inside schools and the district has been a challenge. Complex questions about leadership, roles, expectations, and accountability in the partnership were not easily navigated in an environment where mission, vision, and leadership were different. Where we were able to focus on common agendas and agree on specific projects, we were successful. Where the district lost focus on the centrality of reform as a community-driven process, we struggled with creative tension. Schools in which principals believed in organizing and parent empowerment became powerful partners with good results for their children, found a guardian angel in OCO, and are becoming powerful advocates for ongoing systemic change. Partnership grew thin over time in schools with principals who did not incorporate organizing principles in the culture of their school. Despite this complexity, OCO has demonstrated that there can be effective advocacy and organizing from inside schools and the district. However, there must be buy-in and true support from principals at the site level and from the superintendent at the district level. Also, unless OCO maintains the ability to organize externally, leverage for change and accountability will erode over time.

Phase III: Advocacy in arenas beyond local reach: The power of a model and a network

As we developed our inside-outside strategies, we thought we were on the road to powerful change. Momentum grew through building new schools around a unified vision that provided parents and students a place at the decision-making table and included them in the redesign of the district administration to support school autonomy and accountability, parent and student empowerment, and choice. Then we ran into a major obstacle: discovery too late that the district budget would be overspent by $50 million. Efforts to find ways to borrow against other accounts, reduce the offer of a teacher pay raise, or find other measures to address this gap all failed. In 2003 the state ultimately took over OUSD and put in place a state-appointed administrator. Oakland Community Organizations leaders were frightened that five years of reform work would be taken away because of this single act in Sacramento.

Staff and leaders at OCO quickly developed a strategy to sustain small school reform within this context. In the first six months of 2003, they held sixty action meetings where thousands of people focused on the message, "Do what is right for students." For OCO, that meant tying advocacy for small school reform and its principles to the positive test scores and attendance results for children in the small schools. Emphasizing improved student outcomes increased our leverage. The decision to take over the district had been made, so we knew the target of our efforts had to include specific language in the state takeover legislation that would protect small school reform efforts.

NEW DIRECTIONS FOR YOUTH DEVELOPMENT • DOI: 10.1002/yd

In addition to the sixty local actions, we had several small negotiating meetings and one large action with Senator Perata and the
state superintendent of education, Jack O'Connell, seeking to protect small school reform. And after local actions and negotiating
meetings with a state senator and the state superintendent of education, the state take-over legislation, SB 63, did incorporate language that supported small school reform.

We also understood that although the legislation encouraged the
state administrator to support promising reform efforts like small
schools, it did not mandate him to do anything. With the arrival of
state-appointed administrator Randolph Ward, we set up a meeting to make the case for small schools—how they were getting better results for students, maintaining better attendance, and keeping
more money in the system—as well as offering parent, teacher, and
principal testimony that showed they were on the same page as
advocates for the children. While noncommittal in detail, Ward
delivered the message that he was all about children and that the
mandate he had from the state was exactly what small schools were
doing: getting better academic results for students and saving
money through better attendance.

This set the stage for the district to make the principles of the
small school reform effort the central idea for district-wide reform.
Our partner from earlier days, BayCES, over time developed a
strong working relationship with Ward. Together they raised significant funding to continue small school development and central
administration redesign based on principles of small schools. Over
the course of the next few years, more than thirteen new schools
were designed. The "Expect Success Central Administration
Redesign" began to roll out. At the school site level, OCO worked
with parents at new small schools as they opened and when we
were welcomed by the principal. However, we were not included
in the central administration redesign conversations. The inside-
outside phase had ended, and we were once again on the outside.
Nonetheless, OCO continued to have a profound effect: thirteen
more schools opened with strong parent involvement and opportunity for school site advocacy.

It is important to observe a critical element that enabled OCO to generate the power needed not only to protect the small school reform ideas but expand and make them central to the reform of the entire system. This kind of power comes from the use of a common and consistently applied organizing model. The fact that OCO congregation and school leaders used the same PICO model over years allowed them to move with trust in each other and the organization they created. The use of this model also created the relationships needed to call on PICO California Project support. Because of history, reputation, and internal and external relationships, OCO parents and congregations were able to exercise power that sustained the small schools policy through a period when parents alone would not have had access in these more distant arenas of power. Being part of an organizing network in which there were strong relationships, a common organizing model, and shared democratic and faith values elevated OCO's ability to advocate in an arena where alone we would have been powerless.

Phase IV: Threat from afar: No Child Left Behind

In January 2004, we learned that the administration was proposing a radical and immediate solution to deal with thirteen schools that had reached the point of reconstitution after several years of failure in meeting the benchmarks mandated by No Child Left Behind (NCLB) legislation. Ten of these failing schools were the overcrowded schools where parents had organized to give birth to the new small schools. Oakland Community Organizations had relationships with many parents in these schools through member congregations or previous school work.

Although it was not clear that NCLB required reconstitution (removal of all staff), the administration decided to start its own charter management organization and change most of the failing schools into charters. Part of the motivation for this appeared to be the additional money that was available from the private sector by pursuing this path. This proposal drew strong ire from the Oakland Education Association (OEA) because these schools would be excluded from their contract. The union wanted OCO to stand up for its teachers and oppose the composition as charters. Legally, changing a school to a charter required a majority vote of tenured teachers or a majority vote of parents. Oakland Education Association began to organize teachers to oppose; OCO took a different route.

Oakland Community Organizations once again focused on empowering parents with information and choice. We developed a series of training sessions to explain what NCLB was rather than oppose it. We helped parents understand the legislation as a tool to see if performance expectations were different from their own. Universally parents felt that their children should be able to read and do math at the level suggested by NCLB, and we explored together whether reconstitution or formation as charters were the only or best alternatives. We encouraged parents to look at the formation of new small schools as another alternative. We conducted one relatively small action—two hundred people at a local church—and asked Ward to ensure parent voice in the decision-making process and include new small schools as one of the options. Realizing that the power to make the final decision ultimately rested with him, we framed the issue around what was best for children and the need for parents to be part of the decision-making process. He agreed to a process that included a visit to each failing school to hear from parents about their ideas.

Over the next two months, we organized parents to prepare for these meetings and further explored the option of charter formation. Through visits we organized to other small schools, parents discovered that they could be involved in the design of such schools and have a role in their governance, curriculum, and culture. We also encouraged parents to meet with the charter school operators selected by the district to understand their vision for schools. The central idea for these charter organizations was built around tight control of curriculum and scripted work for teachers with the intent to lift low-performing children's test scores. The parents' role was to support the academic work of students and the culture that the principal thought essential to the operation of a school with this focus. Oakland Community Organizations was not opposed and in fact had supported opening a KIPP (Knowledge is Power Program) school that operated with a rigorous environment. OCO was not opposed to a highly scripted program and in fact had supported opening a KIPP school that operated with just such a rigorous environment. What we saw as crucial was that parents had a voice and a choice.

As parents met with Ward or his representatives in follow-up meetings, most schools chose the small school option and petitioned to enter the district's small school incubator to begin redesign. In the end, at two schools the district defined which teachers could vote, and those schools were turned into charters. Two other schools were deemed close enough to the NCLB benchmarks to be provided another year. The rest of the schools were invited into the small schools incubator over the next two years. Parents were pleased with the success of their organizing advocacy. Forty-five schools are now open, and another three schools will open in fall 2008.

In this phase of advocacy, we used NCLB's mandated tools, and the parent choice option was created as a central principle at the district level because of our reform work, turning both to our advantage. We used NCLB to agitate parents to not protect what exists, and we used the choice option to force the district to create real alternatives rather than a one-size-fits-all approach. The tool of exposing contradictions became a lever to protect and advance reform.

Conclusion

We have come full circle. As we find ourselves returning to our starting point, supporting the development of new schools and new facilities, we must be vigilant to develop leaders who build the power of their own organization to protect the interests of their children.

I have described our work over the past ten years and highlighted key lessons learned about advocacy: the centrality of love (self-interest) as a motivator to advocacy; the importance of quality research and powerful ideas (a vision for the future) as alternatives to the status quo; application of a model that creates a common structure, language, and experience to sustain leader trust and loyalty over time; the need for institutional and network power to apply leverage; the flexibility to see and seize opportunity when the window is open; and, finally, faithfulness to the object of our love: our children.

Note

1. The mission of OCO, founded in 1977, is to develop leaders who build a powerful organization, embodying faith and democratic values, to cause change and improve life for our families. Oakland Community Organizations works to unite people across diverse Oakland communities in order to collectively improve the quality of life for families, especially those in greatest need. We envision Oakland as a city in which all people have equal access to a first-rate education; affordable housing and home ownership; skills training and good employment opportunities; quality health care; and safe, clean streets in vibrant neighborhoods. Oakland Community Organizations is a federation of forty congregations and allied community organizations representing forty thousand families from East, West, and North Oakland. It is a member of the PICO National Network, one of the largest grassroots efforts of faith-based organizations in the United States.

RON SNYDER *has organized with PICO network for thirty-five years. In addition to directing OCO, he founded PICO affiliates in two states and the PICO California Project.*

NEW DIRECTIONS FOR YOUTH DEVELOPMENT • DOI: 10.1002/yd

Foundations can fund youth organizing and advocacy across multiple interest areas and assist young people in achieving impressive social, cultural, and personal change.

7

Developing the field of youth organizing and advocacy: What foundations can do

Sylvia M. Yee

THE SAN FRANCISCO BAY AREA is home to a large philanthropic community that provides seed capital for innovation and social change. The region also has a rich history of social and political activism and is well known for its participation in antiwar, immigrant, gay and lesbian, women's, and environmental justice movements. Nourished by this potent mix of commitment to progressive change by both activists and funders, the Bay Area has given birth to some of the most promising and exciting youth development programs in the country.[1] These programs embrace a wide spectrum of strategies, but a growing number of them are distinguished in that they engage young people and their adult allies in authentic and powerful forms of organizing and advocacy.

I extend my appreciation to colleagues for their helpful comments on this article: Taj James, Cheryl Rogers, Darlene Hall, Grant Garrison, Heather Graham, and Ira Hirshfield. And special thanks go to Shambhavi Sarasvati for her skillful editing.

The Evelyn and Walter Haas, Jr. Fund has seeded many Bay Area youth organizing and advocacy programs. For more than a decade, the fund has invested in programs that have yielded significant achievements for individual youth participants and impressive improvements to institutions and social policies affecting the health, safety, education, and economic prospects of young people. Youth organizing and advocacy programs are proving to be particularly transformative for young people from low-income families and traditionally marginalized communities, as such programs encourage more empowering connections to self-identity, cultures, and civic life.

Youth advocacy and organizing programs are relatively new. By reflecting on both the history and the current state of the field, foundations can develop strategies to strengthen an emerging and robust body of work that is ripe for advancement. In this article, I consider why supporting youth advocacy and organizing is a key strategy from the perspective of one local foundation, the Haas, Jr. Fund. I briefly describe our history of support of the Bay Area youth development movement as the larger context for our funding of youth organizing and advocacy, and I describe some exemplary program strategies and achievements developed in the region. Finally, I share a funder's perspective about effective roles that philanthropy can play in supporting a new generation of change makers.

Advocacy and organizing: Key social change strategies for the Haas, Jr. Fund

Founded in 1953, the Evelyn and Walter Haas, Jr. Fund is a family foundation in the San Francisco Bay Area. It is motivated by its founders' vision of a just and caring society in which all people are able to live, work, and raise their families with dignity. Guided by the values of fairness, equality, and opportunity, the fund aims to improve the lives of low-income families and children, revitalize the neighborhoods where they live, and promote equal rights and access, particularly for immigrants and gay and lesbian people.

NEW DIRECTIONS FOR YOUTH DEVELOPMENT • DOI: 10.1002/yd

Community engagement is one of the fund's core values. In each of its program areas, it strives to provide opportunities for people to have a voice and play an active role in community and civic life. Supporting the development of grassroots advocates and organizers has been central to its theory of change since the early 1980s. Listening closely to concerns raised by community-based groups, the fund came to appreciate that a core of politically engaged and savvy activists capable of problem solving, altering power dynamics, and securing significant policy changes is the most important community asset for addressing discrimination, racism, and poverty. Fostering advocates and organizers in marginalized communities strengthens democracy by empowering them to be active agents in shaping both their own futures and the larger public sphere.

A local foundation's role in promoting the growth of the youth development movement in the San Francisco Bay Area

Youth organizing and advocacy programs are emerging from both the youth development movement and larger social and political movements in the Bay Area. Funders have found it useful to reflect on the history and characteristics of the youth development movement since, in many respects, its fundamental paradigm—that of supporting the healthy, individual development of all youth—shapes the more recent youth organizing and advocacy programs. The importance of afterschool youth programs is widely accepted today, but a scant fifteen years ago, this was not the case. In 1992, the Carnegie Corporation's Council on Adolescent Development released *A Matter of Time: Risk and Opportunity in the Nonschool Hours*.[2] The report identified adolescence as a time in which every teenager needs opportunities to develop self-esteem, autonomy, and new skills and participate in meaningful afterschool activities. The Carnegie report marked an exciting moment of paradigm shift. Philanthropy began to move away from an emphasis on "fixing" troubled youth and toward supporting the healthy development of all young people.

Across the country, local foundations absorbed the lessons of the Carnegie Report and began to act on them. In the Bay Area, the Haas, Jr. Fund brought together leaders from influential local groups, such as the Urban Strategies Council in Oakland and Coleman Advocates in San Francisco, with national leaders who helped translate into accessible language the key strategies of this new approach: "Safe places for kids, productive things for them to do, caring adults to relate to." By 1994, with Haas, Jr. Fund support, Coleman Advocates had launched Youth Time, a new initiative that marked a dramatic shift from an earlier focus on crisis intervention toward an emphasis on prevention and healthy youth development.

In Oakland, the fund supported the Urban Strategies Council's 1996 report, *Call to Action: An Oakland Blueprint for Youth Development*.[3] The report made the case for greater local investment in the healthy development of the city's youth and served as a guide and rallying cry for advocates. Armed with the blueprint report and inspired by Coleman Advocates' groundbreaking voter initiative earmarking .025 percent of local property taxes for children's services in San Francisco, Oakland advocates pushed successfully for passage of Measure K, which set aside 2.5 percent of general funds, yielding $72 million over twelve years, for youth development programs in the city.

Since the Haas, Jr. Fund has had a longstanding commitment to youth and promoting community participation and civic leadership, it took an active role in disseminating the new youth development paradigm because it offered a research-based theory and comprehensive way of thinking about what all youth need to become productive adults and the important role that the community can play. It began to support a wide array of new programs offering young people new opportunities to gain sophisticated skills and engage more actively in their communities. During the five years from 2003 through 2007, the fund has made grants totaling nearly $16.5 million to support youth development programs as well as comprehensive strategies aimed at strengthening the public policy and nonprofit infrastructure in order to alter the environment and better support healthy development. In the same period, it invested $4 million targeted specifically toward enabling youth to advocate and organize for solutions to issues of concern to youth and to the fund.

Raising the bar on what youth can do: The rise of youth organizing and advocacy

The seeds planted fifteen years ago in the early days of the youth development movement have sprouted a new generation of Bay Area programs that offer youth opportunities to participate in much higher levels of civic activism. Youth design and implement impressive campaigns focused on making changes in institutions that affect their daily lives such as schools, juvenile justice, health care systems, the media, and foster care.[4] Successful campaigns run the gamut from challenging racist representations of youth of color in the media to winning millions of public dollars for a variety of youth services. Above all, youth advocacy and organizing programs are built on a foundation of an analysis of power and inequalities due to racism, sexism, sexual orientation, and class.[5] Youth organizing and advocacy programs, observes Taj James of the Movement Strategy Center, shift the focus from helping individual youth beat the odds to helping them change the odds for themselves and their communities (Taj James, e-mail to Sylvia Yee, May 3, 2007).

Clearly, however, in the pursuit of policy or social change outcomes, youth organizing and activism programs have not abandoned the broader youth development paradigm with its focus on individual development. Youth organizing and advocacy programs intentionally transfer an impressive array of skills to young people. Hass, Jr. Fund grantees, for instance, train teenagers of color to research, write, and produce radio programs and to plan and implement sophisticated media campaigns. They teach students in inner-city schools how to conduct needs assessments and program evaluations and present their findings to decision makers. Most youth organizing and advocacy programs develop leadership skills by giving youth substantive and meaningful roles in leadership positions in programming and even governance or experience running organizations as staff or board members.[6] In these ways, youth advocacy and organizing has become a potent pathway to social-cultural change and to the development of capable, productive, and efficacious young people.

The history of the Haas, Jr. Fund's involvement with both organizing and the youth development movement has led it to support programs with this dual bottom line: developing young people's individual capacities and advancing social change through collective action. This experience has led it to conclude that these programs impart a sense of agency to youth that can be more deeply life changing than that imparted by more traditional youth programs. This is especially true for young people who face discrimination, as youth organizing and advocacy programs work intentionally to build young people's critical consciousness and connections to their own identity, cultures, and communities.

New spheres of influence for young organizers and advocates

As the youth organizing and advocacy movement begins to mature, its spheres of influence are widening. Some of the most interesting and robust models of youth organizing and advocacy are rendering not only schools but other youth-serving institutions and entire communities more equitable by confronting racism, sexism, economic injustice, and sexual orientation bias. There is evidence that because of its emphasis on social justice, organizing programs are more likely to recruit and retain young people of color, youth who face challenges because of class and sexual orientation prejudice, and hard-to-reach older youth who have been in foster care or the juvenile justice system.[7]

Haas, Jr. Fund grantees offer potent examples of the multiple pathways by which young people become engaged activists, changing public policy and the social-cultural conditions that affect them most. The following typology of youth organizing programs demonstrates how the fund is putting into practice its theory of change by integrating youth development grant making into other program areas and empowering youth to influence a range of issues. The programs described illustrate the diversity of youth organizing and advocacy programs that could be supported by funders, whether or not any particular philanthropic institution has a grant-making focus on youth development or youth organizing.

Issue-based organizing

Some youth organizing and advocacy programs focus on one issue area or on a constellation of subissues organized under a single theme. These types of programs are most likely to attract more resources because the specific issue they promote, such as health reform or criminal and racial justice, appeals to a broader base of supporters beyond youth funders. As a result, these programs tend to have larger budgets than those primarily supported by youth funders.

Californians for Justice Education Fund (CFJ) is a statewide youth advocacy and organizing group promoting racial justice and education reform. CFJ trains low-income immigrant youth and parents to challenge the inadequacy of educational opportunities. Its young people document inequities, conduct media campaigns, develop organizing strategies, and negotiate with local and state officials. By working with the American Civil Liberties Union on the Williams education lawsuit, students participated in winning guarantees that millions of school children in California will have safe, clean schools; qualified teachers; and sufficient classroom learning materials.[8] CFJ is supported through the Haas, Jr. Fund's Education Equity program area; by a major education reform funder, the Hewlett Foundation; by large health foundations concerned with promoting healthy school environments such as California Endowment; and by a number of smaller progressive foundations.

The Gay Straight Alliance (GSA) is an antidiscrimination group working to ensure safe schools for all students, regardless of sexual orientation and gender identity. Through local student-led GSA clubs, the alliance trains students in all aspects of organizing, and students learn how to conduct school climate assessments. The information gathered through these assessments about the impacts of homophobia, name calling, bullying, and all forms of gender expression and sexual orientation bias are used by students to educate and advocate for changes in their schools and communities. GSA receives support from the Haas, Jr. Fund's Gay and Lesbian program area, the Ford Foundation, a major civil rights funder, and smaller progressive donors (Liberty Hill and Columbia Foundations) concerned with gay and lesbian rights.

A third successful example of issue-based organizing with broad foundation support is the Ella Baker Center for Human Rights in Oakland, which trains and mobilizes youth of color who have been incarcerated or otherwise affected by the juvenile justice system. Its young people speak before policymakers, write op-eds and reports about successful community programs, give news interviews, and organize media events to draw attention to its Books Not Bars campaign, which fights to redirect California's resources away from youth incarceration and toward rehabilitation centers and community-based programs. In 2006, California's governor signed one of four bills backed by Ella Baker Center youth activists. The bill (SB 1742) focuses on ensuring adequate staffing and programs for incarcerated youth with special needs, including those who need help recovering from substance abuse. The center receives support from the Haas, Jr. Fund as well as from national progressive and racial justice foundations such as Nathan Cummings and from the California Wellness Foundation, a health program funder.

School-focused organizing and advocacy

Many youth development funders support programs that focus on education-related concerns that students identify. Young people, organizing groups, and youth development funders can easily see the connections between students' future life chances and what happens in schools. For example, Kids First, an Oakland-based group, worked in collaboration with other youth groups to win free bus passes for young people who qualify for free lunches and successfully advocated for the creation of the Academic Peer Mentoring/Counseling program at the multiracial Oakland Technical High School.

NEW DIRECTIONS FOR YOUTH DEVELOPMENT • DOI: 10.1002/yd

Youth Together, another multiracial organizing program in Oakland, successfully advocated for the creation of youth centers on two high school campuses and convinced two campuses to institutionalize youth leadership classes, among other achievements. Equally significant, through a survey of its participants, Youth Together found that the majority of youth participants experienced greater self-reliance, increased confidence in playing an active role in the school community and in their organizing skills, and were better equipped to succeed academically.

The work of school-focused groups illustrates the importance of youth organizing to amplify the voice of the consumer in education. Although this type of work has its basis in social and economic justice analyses, these programs generally receive much of their support from local youth funders, as well as social justice funders.

Multi-issue youth organizing programs within large, multi-issue organizations

Multi-issue programs address both school-related and broader community issues. These broader issues often reflect the mission and interests of the parent organization. Youth organizing programs within larger multi-issue organizations can benefit from greater financial stability, although smaller youth programs within institutions whose missions are not specifically youth focused may be constrained in the scope of the youth-driven projects they are able to develop. Nevertheless, this type of embedded youth program may have the potential for expanded support from the larger world of foundations beyond youth development funders.

Youth Making a Change (YMAC), the youth-led program of Coleman Advocates, a nationally known, highly effective child advocacy organization in San Francisco, trains low-income high school students of color to wage policy campaigns about issues affecting young people citywide. Among other impressive wins, YMAC youth won $175,000 in annual funding for YouthSpace, San Francisco's first youth-run, citywide youth center, and they convinced the Department of Public Health and school district to create wellness centers in seven city high schools and to fund the centers at a cost of $1.4 million.

Asian/Pacific Islander Youth Promoting Advocacy and Leadership (AYPAL), a project of Asian Community Mental Health Services in Oakland, ran a youth-led media campaign about the devastating impact that deportations have on families. As a result, Congresswoman Barbara Lee sponsored a bill that brought attention to the issue. This grantee works with harder-to-reach immigrant youth, and its participants often join forces with other youth organizations to design and implement campaigns. Supported by its parent organization, AYPAL was able to track the positive individual outcomes for youth involved in its organizing and advocacy program for at least a year. Tobacco use was reduced from 12 percent to 2 percent, alcohol use from 22 percent to 15 percent, and the arrest rate fell from 13 percent to 6 percent.[9]

Intermediaries building the field through training and technical assistance

Intermediaries play a critical important role in the youth development field in general and in youth organizing specifically. Intermediaries strengthen the capacity of youth programs and their staff, who are often young and inexperienced, rather than provide direct service. They provide research, technical assistance and training about best practices, program design, evaluation, and organizational development. Support for intermediaries offers foundations a strategic way to advance the practice and effectiveness of many programs through a single grant.

The School of Unity and Liberation (SOUL) is an example of a grantee that provides nuts-and-bolts training in organizing and runs a training program to strengthen the capacity of those who work with young people on a variety of social justice issues. Another grantee, Youth in Focus, provides comprehensive training in research, evaluation, and program planning and development to youth-led and youth-oriented nonprofit organizations serving underrepresented young people. Their trainees work on dozens of social justice projects in areas such as health, education, and juvenile justice.

What youth organizing and advocacy groups say they need

Both funders and those who run youth organizing and advocacy programs are motivated by the desire to catalyze positive outcomes in the lives of young people.[10] For this reason, much foundation funding is focused on the programmatic aspects of the work. Yet youth organizing and advocacy programs argue strongly for the need for greater recognition that multiyear investments in strategic planning, evaluation, financial and other management systems, and the development of its leadership are critical to its long-term effectiveness, sustainability, and ability to grow. Following are some of the special characteristics of youth organizing and advocacy groups and their need for capacity building:

• Most youth organizing and advocacy groups are supported primarily through private dollars. They often do not apply for government funding so that they can maintain an independent, critical voice. As a result, groups are relatively modest in size, with annual budgets of $1 million to $500,000, or less. Even when youth organizing groups are programmatically successful, their infrastructure is often quite fragile, as most foundation funding is restricted to underwriting program costs.

• Unlike other nonprofits, youth organizing and advocacy groups often have young staff and boards. They need help in developing not just the leadership of the youth but also the leadership of the executive director, senior staff, and board members.

• Staff members, usually young adults, play multiple roles that would be challenging even for more seasoned staff: mentor, case manager, curriculum developer, conflict manager, case manager, political strategist and organizer, paralegal, and coach, for example. More staff training and time for reflection, especially with colleagues at other sites and programs, are needed.

• Most youth organizing and advocacy groups are focused on local work: a single school, a neighborhood, or a citywide issue. Leaders are concerned about their weak connections to larger social movements. They are eager to share best practices and participate more fully in developing both their own programs and the field as a whole.

• Youth organizing and advocacy groups want and need resources to conduct long-term evaluations that can determine how graduates from their programs have fared. Groups also need resources to conduct internal program improvement reviews and assess staff development needs in a systematic way.

What foundations can do to strengthen the new generation of youth organizing and advocacy programs

In order for foundations to help youth organizing and advocacy groups, it is important for them to understand the previously discussed needs as well as the external pressures these groups face. There are several ways foundations can facilitate the growth and capacity of such organizations.

Build organizational capacity and leadership

Youth organizing and advocacy groups often feel pressure from foundation funders to expand the number of students served and to deliver quick results despite the fact that ambitious campaigns require multiyear action. Organizing work is labor intensive and demands that youth have skilled adult mentors. Rapid expansion can compromise the quality of entire programs. Furthermore, it is difficult for organizing and advocacy projects to specify in advance, much less promise, what policy outcomes might come out of youth-initiated projects. An organizing campaign unfolds over time, and many factors are outside the young people's control. Foundation staff can help by educating themselves and their boards about the multiple factors that shape successful organizing and advocacy outcomes and by encouraging grantees to have realistic goals and objectives.

Youth organizing and advocacy groups, like other nonprofits, require flexible, multiyear general support to enhance the strength and depth of their programmatic work and the long-term health and sustainability of organizational infrastructure.[11] This is an area of need that program staff and funders often ignore. Foundations can help by asking questions that assess organizational and leadership development needs during the grant review process, requesting specific grant objectives to address those needs, and providing general support or adequate funding for both program and infrastructure needs. Long-term and flexible investments to build organizational capacity are required if funders want grantees to realize robust and sustainable impacts.

Some youth organizing and advocacy program executives see themselves more as community or movement leaders than as organizational leaders.[12] As Deschenes, McLaughlin, and Newman argue in the first article in this volume, youth organizing and advocacy groups are a particular breed of organization that operate in a special space between social movements and the mainstream. Traditional organizational assessments and consultants are not always the best match for these groups. Funders need to listen closely and learn along with grantees about the best ways to build capacity.

Make a better case for youth organizing and advocacy

While some youth organizing and advocacy groups receive support from national funders such as the Hazen Foundation, the Surdna Foundation, the Jewish Fund for Justice, and the Open Society Institute, most rely on local support and operate at the margins of philanthropy. Some foundations have not chosen advocacy or organizing as part of their theories of change. Others are concerned that young people are being manipulated by the political agendas of organizations and adult staff. Youth organizing groups struggle to make their case to foundations whose boards are often uneasy with the unpredictable messiness and politically contentious nature of the work.

Foundation staff can address some of these concerns by conveying a better story to foundation boards about the frequently impressive outcomes of youth organizing and its dual bottom line, the quality of the training and mentoring, the ways in which youth organizing and advocacy can add value to multiple program areas, and the invaluable lessons learned from both successes and failures. Site visits with trustees and senior staff of foundations, or youth panel discussions at board meetings, can help bring to life the remarkable personal and social change achievements of young people, as well as the victories of youth organizing.

Fund youth organizing across program areas

Foundations that do not have a youth development or community organizing grant-making priority could consider supporting youth organizing in other priority program areas such as civic participation, education reform, neighborhood revitalization and safety, leadership development, environmental justice, health access, and human and civil rights. Youth organizing is a way to develop young activists in issue areas that funders care about. Care should be taken, however, to balance social change goals with the developmental outcomes for the young people involved.

Support intermediaries

In addition to supporting individual youth organizing groups, foundations can play a critical role by funding the development of infrastructure for the field, particularly by building the capacity of the intermediaries and technical assistance providers who support the knowledge development, dissemination of best practices, convening, training, and consulting for both programmatic and organizational development needs. Intermediaries can also play a useful regranting role for large funders that are constrained in their ability to directly support groups with smaller budgets.

Forge connections

Funders can play an important non-grant-making role by connecting local advocacy efforts to each other and larger networks. A number of important connecting functions are needed: peer learning and exchange; the networking of programs to craft joint action agendas; connecting local community organizing groups with advocacy groups at the regional, state, and national levels; and promoting alliances among youth organizing and advocacy groups and more established, multiconstituency, issue-based groups.

A time for growing and investing

Youth organizing and advocacy is not merely an interesting add-on to the larger world of youth development. It is a pathway to engagement that transforms the lives of young people, especially those who are alienated or marginalized. It is proving that young people can play much more significant roles than previously thought in shaping the institutions that shape their lives. It is opening up a new field of social activism and nurturing a new generation of activists and leaders. Above all, youth organizing and activism is contributing to the preservation and expansion of our democracy by bringing new hearts, hands, and minds into the public sphere.

Youth organizing and advocacy still comprise a relatively small number of programs in comparison to the larger world of youth development. But the number of programs is increasing, and existing programs are developing more sophisticated and robust strategies for engaging young participants. The emergence of youth organizing and advocacy intermediary organizations is evidence that the field is maturing. The time is ripe for foundations to step up and provide critical programmatic and capacity-building support. By deepening its understanding and helping to develop the programs and capacities of this new field, the philanthropic community can enable youth organizing and advocacy to fulfill its promise and play an important role in bringing about a more vibrant, diverse, and effective culture of democracy.

Notes

1. Pintado-Vertner, R. (2004). *The West Coast story—The emergence of youth organizing in California.* New York: Funders' Collaborative on Youth Organizing.
2. Carnegie Council on Adolescent Development. (1992). *A matter of time: Risk and opportunity in the nonschool hours.* New York: Carnegie Corporation of New York.

3. Urban Strategies Council and Youth Development Initiative Working Group. (1996). *Call to action: An Oakland blueprint for youth development.* Oakland, CA: Urban Strategies Council.

4. The Funders' Collaborative for Youth Organizing documents impressive "youth organizing policy victories" across the country, including those of Haas, Jr. Fund's grantees.

5. Ginwright, S., & James, T. (2002). From assets to agents of change: Social justice, organizing and youth development. In B. Kirshner, J. L. O'Donoghue, & M. McLaughlin (Eds.), *Youth participation: Improving institutions and communities.* New Directions for Youth Development, no. 96. San Francisco: Jossey-Bass.

6. Zimmerman, K. (2004). *Making space making change—Profiles of youth-led and youth driven organizations.* Oakland, CA: Youth Wisdom Project/Movement Strategy Center.

7. Lewis-Charp, H., Cao Yu, H., Soukamneuth, S., & Lacoa, L. (2003). *Extending the reach of youth development through civic activism: Outcomes of youth development initiative.* Takoma Park, MD: Innovation Center for Community and Youth Development.

8. *Williams* v. *State of California,* Case No. 312236 (Cal. Sup. Ct, August 14, 2000).

9. Lau, G. (2007, June 27). *AYPAL youth survey.* Progress report submitted to the Haas, Jr. Fund.

10. Based on conversation on Feb. 27, 2007, with Kim Acevos, executive director, Youth Together; Taj James, executive director, Movement Strategy Center; and José Luis, director, Youth Making Change (YMAC), a program of Coleman Advocates. Many of these ideas also emerged from the Ford Foundation's Youth Leadership for Development Initiative, the Roots Initiative of the Funders' Collaborative for Youth Organizing, and a convening by the W. Clement and Jessie V. Stone Foundation of youth programs in October 2006, facilitated by the Innovation Center for Community and Youth Development. (See www.info.wcstonefnd.org.)

11. Buechel, K. W., Keating, E. K., and Miller, C. (2007). *Capital ideas: Moving from short-term engagement to long-term sustainability.* Hauser Center for Nonprofit Organizations, Harvard University, and Nonprofit Finance Fund. http://www.nonprofitfinancefund.org/docs/2007%20May%20onward/Capital%20Ideas/proceedings%20web.pdf.

12. Ryan, B. (2006, March 20). *Unpublished flexible leadership evaluation.* Panel presentation at the Haas, Jr. Fund, San Francisco.

SYLVIA M. YEE *is vice president of programs of the Evelyn and Walter Haas, Jr. Fund in San Francisco.*

Index

Academic Peer Mentoring/Counseling program (Oakland Technical High School), 116

Advocacy: Evelyn and Walter Haas, Jr. Fund approach to, 109–118; faith-based organizing for, 99–100; forging connections for, 122–123; Gates Foundation contribution to, 100; identifying and filling needs of, 119–120; using intermediaries for training and technical assistance, 118, 122; issue-based, 115–116; school-focused, 116–117; strategies for foundations to strengthen, 120–123; student leadership and, 48–50. *See also* Parents; Youth advocate organizations; Youth organizing

Advocate Alert (Coleman Advocates), 73–74

Alinsky, S., 29

Annenberg Institute for School Reform, 56

Asperger's syndrome, 85–86

AYP (adequate yearly progress) [NCLB]: Philadelphia school achievement of, 43; YUC questioning of, 43–44

AYPAL (Asian/Pacific Islander Youth Promoting Advocacy and Leadership) [Oakland], 118

Baker, E., 29, 35–36, 63

BAP (Baltimore Algebra Project): ABC plan proposed by, 37; background of, 35–36; Freedom Fall campaign success by, 37–38; political strategies of, 36–37; student mobilization and outcomes of, 36; successes of, 38–40

BayCES (Bay Area Coalition for Equitable Schools), 99, 100, 103

BCPSS (Baltimore City Public School System), 35

Bill and Melinda Gates Foundation, 100

Books Not Bars campaign (Ella Baker Center), 116

BPON (Boston Parent Organizing Network), 78, 81

BPS (Boston Public Schools), 33, 77–78

BPS School Committee meetings, 77

Bradford v. Maryland State Board of Education, 35

Brodkin, M., 62, 65, 66, 69

Brown, J., 99

Brown v. Board of Education of Topeka, Kansas, 37

Budget 4 Families Campaign (Coleman Advocates), 70

Building Bridges: Linking Child Advocacy and Community Organizing Strategies (Richart), 68

Call to Action: An Oakland Blueprint for Youth Development (Urban Strategies Council), 112

Carnegie Corporation's Council on Adolescent Development, 111

Castlemont High (Oakland), 101

CBOs (community-based organizations): core principles of, 80; description of, 77–78. *See also* JP-POP (Jamaica Plain Parent Organizing Project)

CFJ (Californians for Justice Education Fund), 115

Chaconas, D., 100

Children's Amendment (San Francisco), 62, 66

Children's Defense Fund, 28

128   COMMUNITY ORGANIZING AND YOUTH ADVOCACY

93–94; phase 1: planting the seeds for a movement, 96–100; phase 2: partnership as advocacy approach, 100–102; phase 3: advocacy by using power of model and network, 102–104; phase 4: No Child Left Behind issue, 104–106
OCO (Oakland Community Organizations): advocate educator roles by, 21; approach to rhetorical opposition by, 15–16; demographic context considered by, 96; education reform approach of, 93–94, 96–106; empowerment focus of, 13; faith-based organizing strategy used by, 99–100; local context agenda and work by, 21–23; relationships and coalitions formed by, 18–19; specific proposals and concrete actions by, 17; strategies used by, 14; understanding parent organizing in urban context by, 94–95
O'Connell, J., 103
OEA (Oakland Education Association), 104, 105
O'Malley, M., 37
"Our Schools, Our Superintendent" (Coleman campaign), 70

Parents: becoming involved in JP-POP, 81–84; building collective moral leadership of, 89–90; building knowledge, support, and confidence through JP-POP, 84–89; communication between educators and, 82–83; IEP (individual educational plan) role of, 82, 87–88; language/cultural barriers to communication, 82–83; "legitimate peripheral participation" by, 88; planting seeds for education reform activism by, 96–100; tradition participation in schools by, 79–80; understanding urban context of organizing, 94–95. See also Advocacy; Youth
PAY (Parent Advocates for Youth), 66–67
PDD-NOS (Pervasive Development Disorder-Not Otherwise Specified), 85

Perata, D., 99, 103
Philadelphia School Reform Commission, 43
PICO California Project, 104
PICO (Pacific Institute for Community Organizing), 13, 19, 80, 95, 104
Proposition J (San Francisco), 66

Quality Education as a Civil Right, 37
Quan, C., 99

Richart, D., 68

St. Elizabeth Parish (Oakland), 99
San Francisco Department of Children, Youth and Their Families, 19–20, 62
San Francisco Foundation, 64
San Francisco's Children's Amendment, 62, 66
San Francisco's Proposition J, 66
SBU (Sistas and Brothas United), 46, 54, 55–56, 57
SC-YEA (South Central Youth Empowered Thru Action): educational reform proposals by, 49–50; impact of training curriculum of, 53–54; relationship building by, 55–56; successful efforts of, 46
Schools: AYP (adequate yearly progress) standard for, 43–44; cultural differences between home and, 83; cultural differences between youth groups and, 50–52; KIPP (Knowledge is Power Program), 105–106; organizing and advocacy focused on, 116–117; traditional parent participation in, 79–80. See also Educators
SFOP (San Francisco Organizing Project): advocate educator roles by, 21; empowerment focus of, 13; local context agenda and work by, 21–23; range of action by, 20; relationships and coalitions formed by, 18–19; specific proposals and concrete actions by, 17; strategy used by, 14
Shah, S., 2, 6, 43, 59
Shirley, D., 3, 7, 77, 91
Snyder, R., 3, 8, 93, 107